INTRODUCING
ISSUES WITH
OPPOSING
VIEWPOINTS®

Prescription Drugs

M. M. Eboch, Book Editor

GREENHAVEN
PUBLISHING

Published in 2021 by Greenhaven Publishing, LLC
353 3rd Avenue, Suite 255, New York, NY 10010

Copyright © 2021 by Greenhaven Publishing, LLC

First Edition

Articles in Greenhaven Publishing anthologies are often edited for length to meet page requirements. In addition, original titles of these works are changed to clearly present the main thesis and to explicitly indicate the author's opinion. Every effort is made to ensure that Greenhaven Publishing accurately reflects the original intent of the authors. Every effort has been made to trace the owners of the copyrighted material.

Library of Congress Cataloging-in-Publication Data

Names: Eboch, M. M., editor.
Title: Prescription drugs / M. M. Eboch, book editor.
Description: First edition. | New York : Greenhaven Publishing, 2021. |
   Series: Introducing issues with opposing viewpoints | Includes
   bibliographical references and index. | Audience: Grades 7–12.
Identifiers: LCCN 2019057338 | ISBN 9781534507258 (library binding) | ISBN
   9781534507241 (paperback)
Subjects: LCSH: Medication abuse—United States—Juvenile literature. |
   Prescription pricing—United States—Juvenile literature.
Classification: LCC RM146 .P735 2021 | DDC 615.5/8—dc23
LC record available at https://lccn.loc.gov/2019057338

Manufactured in the United States of America

Website: http://greenhavenpublishing.com

Contents

Chapter 3: How Do Legal Drugs Contribute to Health Problems?

Foreword

Indulging in a wide spectrum of ideas, beliefs, and perspectives is a critical cornerstone of democracy. After all, it is often debates over differences of opinion, such as whether to legalize abortion, how to treat prisoners, or when to enact the death penalty, that shape our society and drive it forward. Such diversity of thought is frequently regarded as the hallmark of a healthy and civilized culture. As the Reverend Clifford Schutjer of the First Congregational Church in Mansfield, Ohio, declared in a 2001 sermon, "Surrounding oneself with only like-minded people, restricting what we listen to or read only to what we find agreeable is irresponsible. Refusing to entertain doubts once we make up our minds is a subtle but deadly form of arrogance." With this advice in mind, Introducing Issues with Opposing Viewpoints books aim to open readers' minds to the critically divergent views that comprise our world's most important debates.

Introducing Issues with Opposing Viewpoints simplifies for students the enormous and often overwhelming mass of material now available via print and electronic media. Collected in every volume is an array of opinions that captures the essence of a particular controversy or topic. Introducing Issues with Opposing Viewpoints books embody the spirit of nineteenth-century journalist Charles A. Dana's axiom: "Fight for your opinions, but do not believe that they contain the whole truth, or the only truth." Absorbing such contrasting opinions teaches students to analyze the strength of an argument and compare it to its opposition. From this process readers can inform and strengthen their own opinions, or be exposed to new information that will change their minds. Introducing Issues with Opposing Viewpoints is a mosaic of different voices. The authors are statesmen, pundits, academics, journalists, corporations, and ordinary people who have felt compelled to share their experiences and ideas in a public forum. Their words have been collected from newspapers, journals, books, speeches, interviews, and the internet, the fastest growing body of opinionated material in the world.

Introducing Issues with Opposing Viewpoints shares many of the well-known features of its critically acclaimed parent series, Opposing

Viewpoints. The articles allow readers to absorb and compare divergent perspectives. Active reading questions preface each viewpoint, requiring the student to approach the material thoughtfully and carefully. Photographs, charts, and graphs supplement each article. A thorough introduction provides readers with crucial background on an issue. An annotated bibliography points the reader toward articles, books, and websites that contain additional information on the topic. An appendix of organizations to contact contains a wide variety of charities, nonprofit organizations, political groups, and private enterprises that each hold a position on the issue at hand. Finally, a comprehensive index allows readers to locate content quickly and efficiently.

Introducing Issues with Opposing Viewpoints is also significantly different from Opposing Viewpoints. As the series title implies, its presentation will help introduce students to the concept of opposing viewpoints and learn to use this material to aid in critical writing and debate. The series' four-color, accessible format makes the books attractive and inviting to readers of all levels. In addition, each viewpoint has been carefully edited to maximize a reader's understanding of the content. Short but thorough viewpoints capture the essence of an argument. A substantial, thought-provoking essay question placed at the end of each viewpoint asks the student to further investigate the issues raised in the viewpoint, compare and contrast two authors' arguments, or consider how one might go about forming an opinion on the topic at hand. Each viewpoint contains sidebars that include at-a-glance information and handy statistics. A Facts About section located in the back of the book further supplies students with relevant facts and figures.

Following in the tradition of the Opposing Viewpoints series, Greenhaven Publishing continues to provide readers with invaluable exposure to the controversial issues that shape our world. As John Stuart Mill once wrote: "The only way in which a human being can make some approach to knowing the whole of a subject is by hearing what can be said about it by persons of every variety of opinion and studying all modes in which it can be looked at by every character of mind. No wise man ever acquired his wisdom in any mode but this." It is to this principle that Introducing Issues with Opposing Viewpoints books are dedicated.

Introduction

"We've heard a lot of stories about the high prices that millions of American patients pay, and struggle to pay, for their drugs every month."

—Health and Human Services Secretary Alex Azar

Would you be alive without prescription medication? Most people have had at least one round of antibiotics by the time they are teenagers. Antibiotics are the most common prescription medicine given to children. For a century, antibiotics have cured diseases that used to be deadly. That doesn't mean you definitely would have died without antibiotics, but chances are at least a few of your friends or family members wouldn't be here without the benefit of such medicine.

Antibiotics are only one of many medicines that save lives and keep people healthier and happier. Many young people take regular medication for conditions such as diabetes, asthma, ADHD, or depression. Older adults are even more likely to take prescription medicines. They may need drugs to control conditions such as high blood pressure or high cholesterol.

Meanwhile, people hold out hope for curing or controlling other devastating diseases, such as Alzheimer's and multiple sclerosis. The news brings regular reports of breakthroughs on treating cancer. While we do not have true cures for all forms of cancers, modern pharmaceuticals help fight the disease. Other prescription drugs treat the side effects of cancer drugs, helping patients get through the treatment.

Prescription drugs save and help a lot of lives. It might then come as a surprise that these medicines are mired in controversy. And yet, they're surrounded by not just one controversy, but several.

In the United States particularly, prescription drugs can be so expensive that people can't afford the medicine they need. Even people who have health insurance, which covers some medical costs, may have to pay part of the cost of the drugs they need. Other drugs may not be covered at all by insurance, perhaps because they're experimental. Some people need hundreds or even thousands of dollars every month to pay for their prescriptions. If they can't afford to pay, they get sicker and may die.

Why are these drugs so expensive? If you ask the pharmaceutical companies, they will claim that it's because they must spend so much money on research and development. Paying high prices for medicine, they say, is the only way we'll get new and better drugs. Yet other people claim that drug companies make outrageous profits and are driven by greed. They say these companies manipulate the market to sell new, more expensive medicines, even when the old drugs work just as well. Drug companies may even convince people that normal aging is an illness to be treated with drugs. They advertise drugs by mentioning common problems such as back pain or headaches. Patients see the ads and ask their doctors for the medicine. Doctors may believe the drug is unnecessary, won't work, or doesn't work as well as other treatments. Yet, they may still feel pressured into giving a prescription.

Taking drugs we don't truly need costs people money. It can even lead to new health problems if the drugs have side effects. Taking prescribed drugs can also lead to dependence or addiction. Dependence happens when the body adapts to regularly taking a medication. Stopping the medicine can cause withdrawal symptoms.

Addiction is more serious. Addiction is a disease of the brain that causes people to use substances despite harmful consequences. People can become addicted to prescription drugs. They may start with their own prescription, or they may share or steal someone else's. They may combine the prescription drugs with illegal drugs. Among young adults, the most commonly abused prescription drugs are pain relievers, anti-anxiety drugs, and attention deficit hyperactivity disorder (ADHD) stimulants. Those who misuse the drugs may simply want to relax, feel more alert, or relieve pain. But the consequences of taking these medications incorrectly can be dire. More young adults die from prescription drug overdoses than from overdoses of illegal drugs. Thousands more wind up in emergency rooms each year.

Even when people take medicine exactly as their doctors prescribe, they may be taking far more drugs than they need. The Addiction Center notes, "According to one study, doctors misdiagnosed almost two-thirds of patients with depression and prescribed unnecessary antidepressants." While drugs, including antidepressants, can help and even save people who need them, we may be getting too many of them.

Overprescribing drugs can have severe consequences, as the history of antibiotics proves. Antibiotics changed medical history profoundly and have saved millions of lives, but they only treat bacterial infections. It can be hard to know for sure if a sickness is due to bacteria, a virus, or something else. Doctors used to prescribe antibiotics to many sick patients, even if they weren't sure the drugs would help. This practice has led to antibiotic resistance. Over time, the bacteria have changed in response to the medicine, learning to resist its effects. Many infections are becoming harder—and sometimes impossible—to treat. According to the World Health Organization (WHO), "Antibiotic resistance is one of the biggest threats to global health, food security, and development today."

Prescription drugs are surrounded by controversy. Are modern medicines miracles or disasters? Is the pharmaceutical industry saving our lives or picking our pockets and making us sicker? Does everyone have a right to get the medicine they need at a price they can afford? If so, how can we make that happen? Exploring these issues through research, philosophical discussions, and personal experience can help individuals determine their answer. The current debates are explored in the diverse viewpoints contained in *Introducing Issues with Opposing Viewpoints: Prescription Drugs*, shedding light on this ongoing contemporary issue.

Chapter 1

What Are Possible Problems with Prescription Drugs?

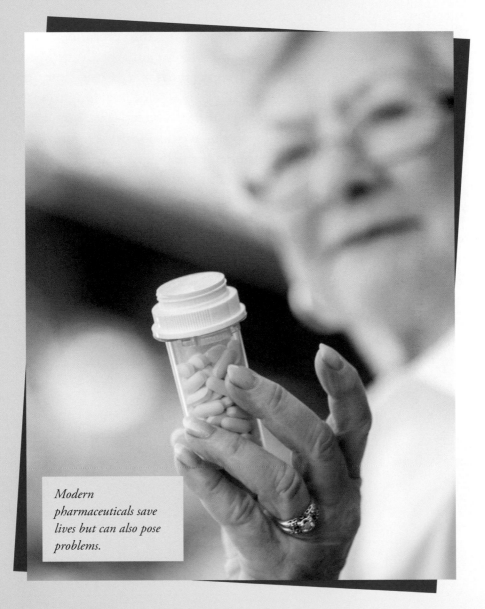

Modern pharmaceuticals save lives but can also pose problems.

Drugs Aren't the Best Way to Treat Pain

Ann Robinson

"Losing the ability to feel pain makes the world a dangerous place. But sometimes pain becomes a chronic problem."

In the following viewpoint, Ann Robinson addresses the challenges of treating chronic pain. She discusses a study that suggests some common pain relievers have harmful side effects. The author lists some alternatives to taking pain relievers. These include physical therapies, such as acupuncture, and mental therapies, such as mindfulness, where people focus their attention and accept what is happening. In addition, maintaining work and exercise can help. However, people with chronic pain often do less and less. In the end, they may rarely leave their home and become isolated from friends. Unfortunately, Robinson writes, taking pain relievers is easy, while other treatments can be expensive or difficult to access. Ann Robinson is a general practitioner and health journalist.

AS YOU READ, CONSIDER THE FOLLOWING QUESTIONS:
1. What is the danger of losing the ability to feel pain?
2. How do our bodies adapt to chronic pain?
3. Why can it be hard for people to get medical help for chronic pain?

The writer and runner Haruki Murakami says: "Pain is inevitable. Suffering is optional." But many of the estimated 28 million people in the UK who live with long-term, chronic pain would beg to differ. Elderly people with back and knee pain become increasingly housebound, withdrawn and socially isolated. Daily nerve pain, headaches or muscle aches lead to depression, unemployment and fractured relationships. And now a study has questioned the safety of commonly used pain-killers diclofenac and ibuprofen after finding an increased risk of cardiac arrest among users. So just what are you supposed to do if you are in pain?

What Does This New Study Say?

Cardiologist and study author Professor Gunnar Gislason of the Danish Heart Foundation says his study underlines existing concerns. "We found there was an increase in sudden cardiac deaths among people on prescribed NSAIDs [non-steroidal anti-inflammatory drugs]; an increased risk of 31% associated with ibuprofen use, and 50% with diclofenac." If you are fit and healthy, the increased risk is unlikely to put you in any danger. But if you are already at high risk, taking NSAIDs is a serious decision that you should discuss with a healthcare professional. Gislason sees it as a major public health issue that needs tackling.

But Dr Alan Fayaz, specialist in pain medicine at University College London, says chronic pain itself can put a strain on the heart, irrespective of NSAID use. Furthermore, people who are prescribed long-term, high-dose NSAIDs are more likely to have other health problems than those that are not, so it can be hard to be certain to what degree the NSAIDs are causing the extra cases of heart attack and stroke. But Fayaz does agree that NSAIDs certainly cause side-effects, including bleeding from the gut and kidney damage, and should be used with caution.

So the Drugs Don't Work?

The experts agree that treating the underlying cause, staying in work, regular exercise and talking therapies are often more

Pain is something everyone has had to address to some degree, whether it was a small headache or debilitating traumatic pain. Which is worse for our health: chronic pain or pain relievers?

successful and less harmful than drugs. The main drugs used for pain control fall into four classes: NSAIDs (eg ibuprofen, naproxen, diclofenac); opioids (codeine, morphine); antidepressants (amitriptyline); and drugs developed for epilepsy (gabapentin, pregabalin). Fayaz says gabapentin can be effective and he favours capsaicin cream—derived from chilli peppers—that can help in fibromyalgia and osteoarthritis. Gislason suggests low-dose naproxen or a weak opioid such as codeine if paracetamol and physiotherapy aren't enough. New preparations, such as Targiniq, aim to minimise the side-effects of opioids (constipation, for example) by combining them with drugs that counter the unwanted effects. In the UK, medicinal cannabis can be prescribed for muscle spasms in multiple sclerosis but not for chronic pain.

Is Pain Ever Good?

Losing the ability to feel pain makes the world a dangerous place. A short-term pain response makes us snatch our hand out of the fire or jump back from an electric shock. Usually, once the cause of pain (trauma, infection or inflammation) has healed, the pain goes away. But sometimes pain becomes a chronic problem. This might be because the underlying cause—a painful ulcer, say—hasn't healed, or the condition recurs (as in migraine) for reasons that no one can fathom. Once pain becomes chronic, it is a devil to treat. Changes in the brain and spinal cord, called central sensitisation, mean you experience more and more pain with less and less provocation. You are more likely to experience chronic pain if you are old, female and live in poor housing. But recovery is possible; two-thirds of those with chronic pain get better over time—although that still leaves an estimated 11% of adults and 8% of children who suffer severe pain.

Can I Avoid Chronic Pain to Start With?

If only. But there are some precautions worth taking. Top up vitamin D levels by getting out in the spring sunshine or considering supplements in the winter; low vitamin D may (arguably) contribute to generalised pain. Back pain and repetitive strain injuries that start in the workplace may be preventable with better work practices. The over-70s can have a shingles jab to reduce the risk of chronic nerve pain that can persist after an attack.

Can Therapy Help?

Pain specialist Professor Anthony Jones, of the University of Manchester, thinks so. "There's good science and evidence behind talking therapies to help to reverse some of the fine tuning problems in the brain that happen in chronic pain. People with osteoarthritis or fibromyalgia anticipate pain differently; they are in a state of permanently expecting bad things to happen to them, including pain." The brain can distract itself from experiencing pain, and functional MRI imaging has shown which parts of the brain are activated when this distraction is taking place. Jones says that new, simple and safe therapies that use the power of the brain to take more control of how we feel are being developed in the human pain research group at the University of Manchester.

Which Talking Therapy Should I Try?

One size doesn't fit all; the best talking therapy is the one with a therapist and philosophy that most appeals to you. The main sticking point is availability. NHS provision is very patchy and there may be a long waiting list. Private therapists may lack proper training and supervision and can charge as much as £100/session. Cognitive behavioural therapy and mindfulness can help. And an interesting mindfulness-based therapy called acceptance and commitment therapy (ACT) says we should accept what we cannot change but can commit to action that improves our lives. You may prefer to take control of your own therapy. The online Pain Toolkit is full of self-management tips and tools. There are apps to track and rate pain and monitor medication use and general wellbeing.

How Can I Distract My Brain?

Western acupuncture, Tens machines (which deliver a small electrical current to the skin) and tapping (repeated tapping with your fingertips on specific points on the body) do not have strong scientific evidence, but do no harm. The basic idea is that the brain processes signals from these techniques and "blots out" the pain signals. Currently, the National Institute for Health and Care Excellence (NICE) only recommends acupuncture for chronic tension-type headache and migraine, but many NHS pain clinics offer it as an option for other types of chronic pain including backache. Jones says these techniques may not be better than a placebo, but "placebo analgesia is one of the most powerful ways of 'tricking' the brain to take more control of pain and can be long lasting."

Are There Pain Specialists I Could Go To?

Your GP can refer you to a specialist pain clinic if you have persistent, disabling or progressive pain despite treatment. If you have become dependent on alcohol, drugs and strong painkillers (opiates), you will need specialist care to wean yourself off. Pain clinics can offer a wide range of options including physiotherapy, psychological support, medication, pain-relieving injections of local anaesthetic or steroids and acupuncture.

I Don't Mind Being a Guinea Pig. Are There Any Trials I Can Sign Up To?

The ReActiv8 study is a trial recruiting volunteers to see whether a novel device helps chronic low back pain. ReActiv8 is a surgically implanted device that uses mild electrical stimulation to activate the large muscles on either side of the backbone for 30 minutes, twice a day. You control when to start and stop each stimulation session via a handheld wireless remote control. The idea is that over time, your body regains control over the muscles that provide lower back stability, which may help relieve chronic low back pain.

Advertising Prescription Drugs on TV Is Dangerous

"The only goal of these commercials is to prompt patients to initiate conversations with physicians."

Milton Packer

In the following viewpoint, Dr. Milton Packer discusses drug ads on TV. He notes that these have become very common, and they often feature rare diseases. The ads may lead patients to talk to their doctors about the medicine advertised. This can lead to unnecessary doctor visits, as the patient worries about a disease they do not have. It can also interfere with the relationship between the physician and the patient. The author then suggests ways to discourage pharmaceutical companies from advertising drugs. Milton Packer is a cardiologist who researches heart failure.

AS YOU READ, CONSIDER THE FOLLOWING QUESTIONS:
1. Why do pharmaceutical companies advertise drugs for rare diseases?
2. Why might a doctor prescribe a drug at a patient's request, even if the doctor doesn't think the drug is needed?
3. Why can't ads for prescription drugs be banned?

"How to Stop Direct-to-Consumer Prescription Drug Ads," by Milton Packer, MedPage Today, LLC, May 23, 2018. Reprinted by permission.

I rarely watch television, but when I do, I am overwhelmed by the number of direct-to-consumer commercials about prescription drugs.

The ads saturate the airways. In a single hour, it is possible to see six different drugs promoted.

Each commercial has a predictable formula. An actor plays the role of a patient afflicted with a certain disease—often one that is exceptionally uncommon and not recognizable by the general public, or by many physicians.

The beginning of the ad superficially establishes the burden of the disease. An actor playing the role of the patient is sad and unable to engage in normal activities. But magically, following a description of the drug, the actor is now happy, active and surrounded by doting family members. The scenes are idyllic, and the music is uplifting.

The commercial ends with the required warnings, precautions and list of adverse events. The information is legally required, but it is not possible to understand what the risk-to-benefit relationship might be. Or what the drug costs.

There is always the central message: "Ask your doctor about ..."

Sounds noble? Not really.

The pharmaceutical industry might claim that these ads are intended to raise awareness, but the general public is not the intended audience. The only goal of these commercials is to prompt patients to initiate conversations with physicians.

Which doctor should that be? Your primary care physician? Many (maybe most) of the diseases being discussed are not treated in primary care.

In fact, ads often prompt unnecessary physician visits, especially when people do not have the disease that the commercial refers to.

Even if the patient actually has the disease and initiates the conversation, the physician may never have heard of the drug. This seems likely given the highly specialized nature of many of these pharmaceuticals.

Perhaps the physician is aware of the drug but does not think it is appropriate for the patient. Does the patient now wonder if the physician is out of touch with recent developments?

Direct-to-consumer pharmaceutical advertisements suggest that carefree days are just a few pills away. They plant seeds in consumers, setting off a potentially dangerous chain of events.

Often physicians might tell patients they are not comfortable prescribing the drug. It is new, and they have limited experience with it, and thus, do not know how to administer or monitor its use. What happens then?

And is it possible that some physicians might refuse to prescribe the drug because they are just annoyed at the pharmaceutical company for placing the ad and believe that it undermines the patient-physician relationship?

Regardless of the circumstances, the commercial is not informative; in fact, it is disruptive. But of course, that is its whole intent.

The FDA first allowed the practice of direct-to-consumer advertising in 1997, and since then, the number of TV commercials for prescription drugs has skyrocketed. Interestingly, only the United States and New Zealand allow for direct-to-consumer advertising for pharmaceuticals. The remainder of the world thinks it is inappropriate.

According to a February 2017 article in the *Los Angeles Times*, drug companies spend more than $5 billion a year pitching prescription medications directly to consumers. That is obscene. Industry spending on direct-to-consumer advertising is now comparable to its spending on marketing to physicians.

Studies report that consumers often place unwarranted trust in these TV prescription drug ads. Practitioners report being bombarded by patient requests, and many feel pressured to prescribe drugs that have been requested by patients, even if they believe it is inappropriate to do so. And the conversation often wastes the limited time the physician has allotted to the patient visit.

Think the situation is bad now? A year ago, pharmaceutical companies were seeking FDA permission to use direct-to-consumer advertising to promote off-label use of drugs for nonapproved indications.

What?

The FDA does not allow pharmaceutical companies to market drugs directly to physicians for non-approved indications. But might they allow companies to tell patients about such use? What purpose could that serve? What kind of patient-physician conversations would that lead to?

I condemn the current pricing structure that the pharmaceutical industry currently utilizes to determine the cost of most innovative products. Drug companies say that they must cover their research and development costs. But obviously, these revenues must also cover the considerable costs of TV advertising.

Several years ago, I stopped working with a pharmaceutical company specifically because of a profound disagreement about their efforts related to direct-to-consumer TV advertising.

I want to be clear. I strongly favor giving patients the information that they need to make informed decisions, but direct-to-consumer advertising for prescription drugs is not about patient empowerment. It is not about providing clarity, and it often does not enhance the physician-patient relationship. It undoubtedly contributes to the high prices of drugs.

Can direct-to-consumer advertising for prescription drugs be banned? Apparently that is legally difficult. The courts have ruled that product advertisements are a form of commercial free speech protected under the principle that a manufacturer has the right to market its products.

So here is a proposal to curtail direct-to-consumer advertising for prescription drugs—legally. Right now, when a pharmaceutical company advertises, it is required to describe the major adverse effects of the drug. I would add two simple additional requirements.

First, I would require manufacturers to describe the size of the expected benefit. This can be a statement of the placebo-corrected effect on the primary endpoint of the pivotal trial(s) that led to approval. Second, I would require manufacturers to tell the public how much the drug costs. This should be the list price, not the discounted price (which companies do not disclose anyway).

Who could possibly argue that such information would not be extremely useful?

My prediction: Implementation of these two requirements would dramatically curtail direct-to-consumer advertising of prescription drugs. Drug manufacturers might hesitate to publicly disclose that many new drugs provide only modest effects or benefit only a small fraction of patients, even though they may be priced at more than $200,000 per year.

EVALUATING THE AUTHOR'S ARGUMENTS:

In this viewpoint, author Milton Packer suggests a way to discourage pharmaceutical companies from advertising drugs on TV. Do you think this is a necessary step? Should companies have the right to advertise whatever they want, however they want? Why or why not?

Drug Companies Create and Market Diseases

"Studies show that pharmaceutical industry 'normal' business is characterized by persistent deceit."

Michael Walsh

In the following excerpted viewpoint, Michael Walsh discusses another concern with drug company advertising. He argues that drug companies actually invent new diseases. They may take a normal life experience and convince people that it is a disease that should be treated with new drugs. For example, as people age, they might have less energy. Drug companies tried to convince men that any change in energy levels must be due to low testosterone. Drug companies have also tried to get people to take medications for mild symptoms. Yet taking drugs can be costly, and the drugs may have side effects that are worse than the condition being treated. Michael Walsh is a New York City–based writer and editor who works for Yahoo News.

AS YOU READ, CONSIDER THE FOLLOWING QUESTIONS:
1. What is "disease mongering"?
2. How does a disease-awareness campaign work?
3. How do drug companies use quizzes to manipulate potential patients?

The pharmaceutical industry's image has been significantly damaged in recent years as the public discovered the role its aggressive marketing played in fueling the opioid epidemic. But the American people are still largely in the dark about what may be pharma's most effective tactic for pushing drugs—marketing diseases.

There's a substantial body of medical literature dating back to the early '90s about the practice known as "disease mongering." Pharmaceutical companies regularly pathologize everyday experiences, convince doctors that they are serious problems, tell a hypochondriacal public it needs help and offers the cure: a new drug. Against the onslaught of billions of dollars in marketing campaigns each year, however, researchers' warnings about these tactics have gone largely unheeded.

To be clear: Pharmacology has helped countless people recover from illness or lead more productive lives. But the number of patients receiving any given drug is often greater than those who would benefit from it, and often includes people it could harm.

The United States was still the largest single pharmaceutical market in 2017, generating more than $450 billion of revenue. In contrast, all of Europe accounted for roughly $214 billion. US pharmaceutical spending alone is double the Organisation for Economic Co-operation and Development average. According to the Mayo Clinic, nearly 70 percent of Americans take at least one prescription drug.

Adriane Fugh-Berman, a professor of pharmacology at Georgetown University Medical Center, said the pharmaceutical industry medicalizes normal life by positing that a vague, highly relatable, everyday condition is symptomatic of a newly invented disease. In other cases, pharma exaggerates the prevalence or severity of an existing condition to entice more customers.

Pharmaceutical company sales representatives may be influencing physicians in irresponsible ways, with the intent to sell more drugs.

"Marketing for a drug can start seven to 10 years before they go on the market. Because it's illegal to promote a drug before it goes on the market, what they're promoting is the disease. That's not illegal to do because there's no regulation on creating diseases," Fugh-Berman told Yahoo News.

Lisa Schwartz and Steven Woloshin, co-directors of the Center for Medicine and Media at Dartmouth Institute for Health Policy and Clinical Practice, said disease-awareness campaigns may seem caring or educational but are often just marketing in disguise. The campaigns often follow three basic steps: lower the bar for diagnosis, raise the stakes so people want to get tested and spin the evidence about a drug's benefits and risks. These steps were seen in campaigns on testosterone deficiency, bipolar disorder and restless leg syndrome.

"Low testosterone was among the biggest cases of disease mongering—a huge increase in prescribing a drug before the benefits and harms of treatment were established," Schwartz said. "And yet, manufacturers claimed 'low T'—not aging or other medical conditions—was the reason why older men might have less energy, worse sports performance or even feeling more tired after dinner than younger men. There are no specific rules about how companies can talk about symptoms in awareness campaigns."

Jack James, a clinical psychologist at Reykjavik University in Iceland, said the image of the pharmaceutical industry as a dynamic global enterprise burgeoning with breakthrough innovations serving the common good is a public relations concoction that obscures the fact that most new drugs are minor variations on existing formulations.

"Most are, at best, expensive marginal improvements on the older and cheaper drugs they are intended to replace, and a substantial proportion of new drugs are more harmful than older formulations. In practice, the emphasis in drug development is on marketing fake innovation rather than genuine innovation," James said.

James's book *The Health of Populations* focuses on the importance of behavioral changes to prevent diseases. He said the cultivation of direct personal relationships between industry representatives and physicians is nearly universal at all levels of private and public health-care. For example, he said, the pharmaceutical industry gives gifts both large (e.g., sponsored trips) and small (e.g., pens and note pads) to encourage particular prescribing patterns—a boon to the industry at the potential cost of harm to the patients, or at best a waste of money by consumers, insurers and the government.

Leonore Tiefer, a sexologist and psychologist at New York University School of Medicine, said the public is susceptible to exploitation by drug companies and thinks the trend will likely continue in the wrong direction.

"I feel that we're still in the ascendant in terms of people expecting more from medicine and therefore being gullible to disease-mongering claims. People are vulnerable and fearful," Tiefer said.

According to a study in the *British Medical Journal*, pharmaceutical companies spend $19 on advertising a new drug for every one dollar spent on the research and development process.

When asked about disease mongering, Mitchell J. Katz, a public affairs specialist at the Federal Trade Commission, said his agency does not have jurisdiction over pharmaceutical advertising and that it's handled by the FDA.

"We also don't 'regulate' advertising, but we do bring action in cases where ads are deceptive, misleading, or the claims they make are not supported by competent and reliable scientific information. But only ads for products within our enforcement jurisdiction," Katz wrote in an email.

Under the Federal Food, Drug, and Cosmetic Act, the FDA requires that all drug advertisements and promotional labeling include a brief summary of side effects, effectiveness and indications of when the drug should not be taken. The FDA prohibits ads from omitting relevant facts, including misleading information or failing to present a fair balance between effectiveness and risks. But promotional material that does not actually mention prescription drugs would not fall under the FDA's jurisdiction, which is established by Congress.

The FDA has an expedited approval process for drugs that address rare diseases, defined as those that affect fewer than 200,000 people. In some cases, drug companies subdivide common diseases so they can be classified as rare diseases to get expedited approval. More often, though, they do the opposite: broaden the definition of an actual disease that only affects a handful of people to increase the market for a drug to treat it.

In the end, Fugh-Berman said, there's no authority that protects against questionable disease categories in any meaningful way.

Schwartz and Woloshin work to improve communication between doctors and the public by helping both see through the disproportionate fears and hopes created by medical advertising and selective reporting. They note that health conditions occupy a spectrum from clearly sick to clearly well, but there's a large gray area in-between. When does a mildly bothersome experience become the symptom of a disease? In many cases, they said, the pharmaceutical industry draws these lines aggressively so the boundaries of normal get smaller and smaller. And they do so unilaterally—no regulators are watching.

"Everyone's legs feel restless now and then, or they feel occasional stinging or burning sensations in their eyes. But far less people have symptoms severe enough to need medical treatment. The problem is that manufacturers increasingly target people with mild symptoms in order to turn them into patients. Unfortunately, treatment may offer little benefit and may not outweigh side effects, cost and inconvenience," Woloshin said.

Woloshin said pharmaceutical company print or online advertisements sometimes feature quizzes that include symptoms associated with a condition, but which the drug did not help in clinical trials.

"Consumers naturally think, 'I see the list of things on this quiz. The drug must treat these things,' even though it doesn't. It's a trick," Woloshin said.

My interviews for this article suggest that the public should be skeptical about quizzes for diseases, as they are often unreliable and ask leading questions meant to convince healthy people they suffer from a newly discovered ailment.

Schwartz and Woloshin wrote an article for the *JAMA Internal Medicine* journal on how the low T campaign was essentially a template for how diseases are sold. Are you a middle-aged man who sometimes feels tired? Has your athletic ability declined at all since your early 20s? Well, that used to be called aging. But these unvalidated online quizzes might suggest you suffer from low T. Lucky for you, Abbott Laboratories manufactures Androgel.

"I think social media can be a disaster for blurring the line between marketing and public health. The marketing world is trying to get more and more companies to do disease-awareness on Facebook since they can tell stories and directly interact with people," Schwartz said. "These sites give you the feeling that someone out there is just trying to help you and give credence to your suffering—not that a company is trying to sell a drug."

Fugh-Berman recalled taking an online test with her coworkers at PharmedOut, a group she directs at Georgetown that exposes pharmaceutical marketing and promotes evidence-based prescribing. The test on pseudobulbar affect (PBA), which manifests when specific brain damage leads to laughing or crying that is inappropriate and unconnected to a person's emotions, suggested that normal human expressions could be signs of PBA with questions like "Do you ever find things funny that other people don't find funny?" and "Do you cry easily?"

"Almost every woman failed. Only one woman passed. Most of the men failed, but more of them passed. I would say that anyone who passed the test I was actually worried about," Fugh-Berman said.

PharmedOut's research focuses on the effectiveness of continuing medical education (CME) funded by the pharmaceutical industry, as well as contrived or exaggerated diseases. She said pharmaceutical companies get doctors on their advisory boards and pay them to educate other influential doctors at CME events. These thought leaders also sign their names to articles—whether written by them or not—so that the company's views find their way into medical literature. When drugs are approved and diseases are accepted as treatable, medical students are then taught to treat what were once considered benign conditions.

"The trouble is that people are very reluctant to believe that things that sound so scientific and medical and are promoted so aggressively by scientific and medical experts could be mythical or at the very best exaggerated," Tiefer said. "People don't want to believe that."

James said private and public interests are so entangled in the health care industry's research infrastructure that it undermines the integrity of scientific research ostensibly conducted for public benefit.

"Studies show that pharmaceutical industry 'normal' business is characterized by persistent deceit, ranging from subtle image manipulation to outright and frequent research fraud," James said. "Individual researchers, who may have the best of intentions but whose work is conducted in collaboration with industry, are subject to a variety of biasing influences."

Self-serving bias, an unconscious process in which judgments, decisions and conclusions favor personal interests over the general good, is chief among these cognitive blind spots. James said these sorts of cognitive biases affecting researchers are nearly impossible to regulate through ethical-conduct codes or public disclosure of conflicts.

"Despite irrefutable evidence of extensive patient harm, years of attempts to prevent harm due to conflicts of interest have failed dismally," James said.

Cindy Pearson is the executive director of National Women's Health Network (NWHN), which came into being 40 years ago. Many women had been given drugs they didn't need or were never told the truth about the drugs they were taking. Although drug mongering affects men too, she said, women are more likely to be targeted partly because they are often the health-care decision makers for their families, keeping abreast of what's new and making sure their families meet recommendations for hygiene, vaccinations and medical tests.

She said the NWHN looks at claims of new conditions very skeptically and is willing to tell women, "Don't believe the hype about this new drug, don't believe the hype about this supposed under-recognized condition and don't rush to get a screening test you've been told is new and can help you."

"I feel that there are people involved in creating new diseases and promoting drugs that aren't really needed who are pretty amoral. Their measurement of success for themselves is strictly sales," Pearson said. "There are good-spirited and good-hearted people in companies who are proud of developing something that provides help to some people—and then their marketing department gets ahold of it and turns it into something else."

[...]

According to James, prescription drugs are responsible for more harm than both surgery and health care–acquired infections. Though it's difficult to measure the full extent of prescription-fueled harm, successive studies show that it has been growing.

"For example, estimates of the extent of harm in the United States published by the Institutes of Medicine in 2000, which at that time were considered so shocking as to be disbelieved by some authorities, have since been consistently eclipsed by new and more detailed analyses," James said. "Recent studies show that harm caused by prescription drugs alone exceeds that which was previously thought to represent the total of health care–related harm from all causes."

The Pharmaceutical Research and Manufacturers of America and the Biotechnology Innovation Organization, the top trade groups for the pharmaceutical industry in the US, did not respond to requests for comment.

EVALUATING THE AUTHOR'S ARGUMENTS:

In this viewpoint, author Michael Walsh accuses drug companies of "disease mongering." How does he support this accusation with statistics and expert opinions? Why would drug companies want to market new drugs to people who don't need them? What, if anything, should be done about this issue?

Drugs Can Build Up to Dangerous Levels

"There is a tendency for physicians to prescribe a medication for every symptom, and not every symptom requires a medication."

Mary A. Fischer

In the following viewpoint, Mary A. Fischer discusses drug toxicity. This is a common problem, especially in older patients. However, doctors often miss the connection between the symptoms a patient presents and their drug levels. Instead of suspecting toxicity, they may diagnose a new illness entirely. This can lead to new prescriptions and an even higher chance of drug toxicity. Tests can check for drug toxicity, but these tests are not commonly done, and the results may be misread. Patients can help avoid drug toxicity by carefully reading drug safety information and by making sure their doctors know all the medicines they're taking. Mary A. Fischer is a writer and editor whose work has appeared in the *Atlantic*, *Pacific Standard*, and *Men's Journal*.

"When Medicine Makes You Sick," by Mary A. Fischer, American Association of Retired Persons, Sept./Oct. 2010. Reprinted by permission.

AS YOU READ, CONSIDER THE FOLLOWING QUESTIONS:
1. What changes can lead to drug toxicity?
2. How can visiting several doctors lead to drug toxicity, and how could sharing electronic medical records help avoid the problem?
3. How does age affect drug toxicity?

Los Angeles civil attorney Lisa Herbert (not her real name), 61, was shopping at Trader Joe's one evening in June 2009 when she suddenly became disoriented. For an hour she wandered the aisles in a haze, filling her cart with chocolate cupcakes and frozen tamales. At home she talked incessantly, yelled at her roommate, and—convinced she had found an ingenious way to clean the apartment—yanked a fire extinguisher off the wall and sprayed the kitchen and bathroom with a thick white foam.

By morning Herbert's mental clarity had returned, along with a deep embarrassment and confusion over what had caused such bizarre behavior. The answer—which her ever-vigilant doctor immediately suspected—was drug toxicity, a gradual buildup of prescription medication in her bloodstream.

Herbert, who has multiple sclerosis, had been taking baclofen for the past six years to control muscle spasms in her legs. She had taken the same dose all that time with no ill effects, but three months before her disorienting episode, she had begun a strict, low-carb diet and had proudly shed 15 pounds. Because she was thinner yet still taking the same dose of baclofen, the drug had built up to toxic levels.

Drug toxicity is a common and significant health problem, yet it often goes undetected by both patients and doctors, who don't suspect it as the cause of such symptoms as mental disorientation, dizziness, blurred vision, memory loss, fainting, and falls. Although drug toxicity may result when a medication dose is too high, it can also happen because a person's ability to metabolize a drug changes over time or, in the case of Herbert, because she simply didn't need as much of the drug at her lower weight.

Older people are at high risk for drug toxicity, but younger people can suffer symptoms as well. Drug toxicity is "a major public-health

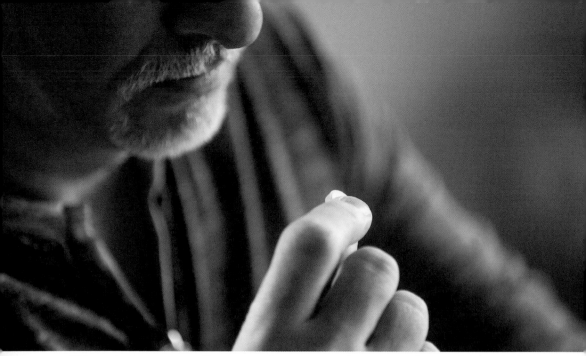

Older patients are prone to drug toxicity. It is important for patients to keep careful records of the medications they are taking and to communicate that information to their physicians.

issue even for people in their 40s and 50s," says Mukaila A. Raji, M.D., chief of geriatric medicine at the University of Texas Medical Branch in Galveston. "Most drugs are eliminated from the body through the kidneys and liver, but starting around the fourth decade we start accumulating fat and lose muscle mass, accompanied by a progressive decline in the ability of our kidneys and liver to process and clear medications. All of this makes us more prone to drug toxicity." According to findings from the Baltimore Longitudinal Study of Aging, age-related loss of kidney function often starts even earlier, in your 30s, and gets worse with each passing decade.

Despite the well-established connection between aging and drug toxicity, physicians sometimes fail to equate patients' symptoms with an adverse drug reaction, attributing them instead to a new medical condition. "As doctors, we see a lot of patients who come in with a general 'I don't feel well' complaint, or maybe they're confused and dehydrated, and we attribute it to a viral illness, when it's caused at least in part by the medication they're taking," says medical toxicologist Kennon Heard, M.D., an associate professor at the University of Colorado School of Medicine in Denver.

Physicians' prescribing habits may also be partly to blame. "There is a tendency for physicians to prescribe a medication for every symptom, and not every symptom requires a medication," says Raji. The more medications a patient takes, the more likely one of them will build up to toxic levels, experts say.

Finally, patients often see multiple doctors who do not communicate with one another and so end up prescribing similar drugs—which, when combined, can reach toxic levels. Electronic medical records will help close the communications gap, experts say. Computerized Clinical Decision Support Systems—used by many hospitals to generate patient-specific recommendations for care—will also help. A 2005 *Journal of the American Medical Association* study of the systems' effectiveness showed improvements in diagnosis, drug dosing, and drug prescribing.

To avoid drug toxicity, patients should be proactive by keeping a careful record of which drugs they're taking—including over-the-counter medications—and bringing that list to every doctor visit.

They can also insist that their doctors consider drug toxicity when a new symptom arises. "Many doctors don't specifically test for drug toxicity," explains Raji, "and a simple CBC [or blood chemistry panel] won't detect it." Certain blood tests can monitor the levels and effects of several drugs, including levothyroxine (Synthroid), warfarin (Coumadin), some antibiotics, and digoxin (Lanoxin). But even so, says Raji, "the blood range of digoxin that's listed as 'normal' in medical textbooks is based on tests done on young people." In general, say medical experts, the best way to determine if drug toxicity has occurred is to eliminate or reduce the dose of a suspected medication when safe to do so—as Lisa Herbert's doctor did.

Patients should also read the safety inserts that come with their medication—before taking it. After recovering from what she calls her "cognitive flip-out," Herbert finally read her baclofen insert, discovering in the fine print the drug's rare but possible adverse effects:

FAST FACT

Drug toxicity can happen when a patient takes too much of a drug and it builds up in the body. In some cases, a normal dose may be toxic for a particular patient.

seizures, confusion, even hallucinations. Had she read the insert earlier, she realized, she might have saved herself and her roommate a good deal of anguish—not to mention a day's work in cleaning up one very messy apartment.

EVALUATING THE AUTHOR'S ARGUMENTS:

In this viewpoint, author Mary A. Fischer addresses toxic buildup of drugs in the system. Consider previous viewpoints in this chapter that discuss how and why people may wind up taking unnecessary medications. What are the benefits of taking multiple medications? What are the risks? How can individuals and society keep the benefits and risks in balance?

We Must Go Beyond Clinical Trials

"Incorporating real-world data in the drug-development process will lead to safer, more effective drugs and improved health outcomes."

Neile Grayson

In the following viewpoint, Neile Grayson describes some of the problems with clinical trials, which drugs must go through before they are approved. She says that "real-world data" can provide better answers. However, it is not simple to use real-world data. Information may be stored in many places, with limited access. The author suggests that groups should coordinate to make it easier to share health records. This could help with the development of new drugs, as well as other medical improvements. Dr. Neile A. Grayson, Ph.D. is managing director of Health2047, a business that develops health care solutions.

AS YOU READ, CONSIDER THE FOLLOWING QUESTIONS:
1. What is real-world data?
2. How can apps make the sharing of real-world data easier?
3. How can real-world data improve drug development, according to the author?

"Real-World Data Can Help Make Better Drugs and Do It Faster," by Neile Grayson, STATNews.com, May 2, 2018. Reprinted by permission.

Clinical trials have traditionally served as the gold standard for developing and testing new drugs and devices. Relying solely on them to demonstrate safety and effectiveness, though, can be risky. That's why we need greater use of real-world data.

Take, for example, the diet drugs fenfluramine and dexfenfluramine (when combined with phentermine they were commonly known as fen-phen). Data collected *after* they received FDA approval showed a strong association between use of these drugs and cardiovascular problems, and they were ultimately pulled from the market.

The beauty of clinical trials is that they provide a standardized approach to developing a medical treatment within carefully prescribed conditions. The downside is that they focus on highly selective, homogenous populations and provide limited outcome measurements. Incorporating real-world data can help overcome these limitations and mitigate risk. That's why the pharmaceutical industry needs to embrace it more strongly.

What Are Real-World Data?

In health care and drug development, the term "real-world data" refers to information collected beyond the confines of traditional clinical trials. These data can come from electronic health and medical records, billing and prescription databases, insurance claims, disease registries, and more.

Pharmaceutical companies tend to use three types of real-world data:

- Data collected as part of clinical trials, mainly used to supplement the development of a treatment
- Data collected outside of clinical trials, generally used to improve aspects of trial implementation
- Data collected after a treatment is approved and on the market, often used to track long-term safety, tracking market access, and cost-effectiveness

Post-marketing data is the type of real-world data that pharmaceutical companies use most often.

Real-world data might be able to be tracked on apps on personal digital devices.

Real-World Examples

Some large pharmaceutical companies know that collecting real-world data needs to be an integral part of the drug-development lifecycle, from early research through post-marketing activities. They have established internal competencies embedded in existing departments, such as Eli Lilly's Patient Outcomes and Real-World Evidence division. Most companies, though, have not moved beyond using real-world data for post-marketing surveillance and safety monitoring, although several are experimenting with real-world clinical trials earlier in the development process.

In 2016, Boehringer Ingelheim conducted a real-world study examining medical care provided to men with lower urinary tract symptoms. It collected information before an actual clinical trial was started to better understand current medication use and patient behavior, such as how often men visited a physician for this problem, the types of treatment they received, and practice patterns of primary care physicians. It also helped identify patient inclusion and exclusion criteria and guided patient recruitment for a prospective trial. Real-world data were built into the development process before development was begun for a new treatment.

Similarly, the Salford lung study was a pivotal, double-blind study of a novel inhaled therapy for chronic obstructive pulmonary disease developed by GlaxoSmithKline (GSK). The goal of the study was to evaluate the safety and effectiveness of this new therapy in a real-world population of English patients treated by their usual general practitioners. It showed that patients with chronic obstructive pulmonary disease who were treated with the new medication achieved superior reduction in COPD "flares" compared with usual care. It also showed that demonstrating drug effectiveness and safety in a practical clinical setting and in a real-world population provided important high-quality data for clinicians and shorter timelines for studies, thus reducing development costs for new drugs.

Regulatory authorities in the US and Europe believe that real-world data can make the drug-development process more efficient and cost-effective, as well as help better inform patients and physicians about the uses of new products. Last year, the FDA issued final guidance on the use of real-world data for the development of devices, and FDA commissioner Scott Gottlieb has pledged to issue guidance on real-world data for both pre-and post-marketing drug studies. The European Medicines Agency, the European equivalent of the FDA, has provided initial guidance on regulatory approaches to using real-world data in the post-marketing studies it requires.

The Future of Real-World Data

Although there is general agreement in the pharmaceutical industry that it's important to incorporate real-world data into the drug-development process, doing it is easier said than done. The two biggest barriers today are data accessibility and security concerns.

In the US, making it easier to access real-world data would require large-scale aggregation of health data, which are currently stored in multiple silos. One approach would be to link all data collected on an individual, with clear communication about who will have access to the information and how it will be used. Patients would authorize data sharing from apps, physician visits, pharmacy records, lab reports, and the like, creating shareable health records useful for clinical trials. Apple (AAPL) has moved in this direction with a Health app feature that lets patients and providers share pertinent data and interact on iPhones and iPads. As I write this, more than 40 health care organizations support this kind of shareable health record.

Real-world data can also be aggregated at the provider level with incentives in place for data sharing between institutions while ensuring patient confidentiality, such as with the NIH's All of Us research program or Verily's Project Baseline program. The gist of both is to partner with academic and patient groups to safely collect lifestyle and health data on large groups of individuals over long periods of time.

Technical barriers, such as incompatibility between data platforms and data quality issues, currently impede data extraction from electronic health records for secondary uses. But these barriers are likely to be lowered as advances in technology untangle unstructured data and companies develop solutions for merging disparate systems to more effectively collect and analyze health data.

Recent ambitious efforts at capturing and analyzing real-world data have concentrated mostly on broad epidemiologic outcomes or physician-patient communication. Both are important, but drug development should not be overlooked. There is some encouraging movement in this direction. Roche (RHHBY), for example, recently acquired Flatiron Health, an oncology electronic health record firm, partly to facilitate access to regulatory-grade real-world data. Other pharmaceutical companies are also taking initial steps toward harnessing this kind of data.

But the industry needs to move more quickly and decisively. More information leads to better products. Investing in and incorporating real-world data in the drug-development process will lead to safer, more effective drugs; faster and more efficient drug development; and improved health outcomes for everyone.

EVALUATING THE AUTHOR'S ARGUMENTS:

In this viewpoint, author Neile Grayson says we should use more data collected from patients to improve medicine, including drug development. Do you agree with her conclusions? Why or why not? What would have to happen for her suggestions to succeed? Are there concerns that should be addressed, such as patient privacy?

Chapter 2

Why Is Medicine Expensive and Difficult to Obtain?

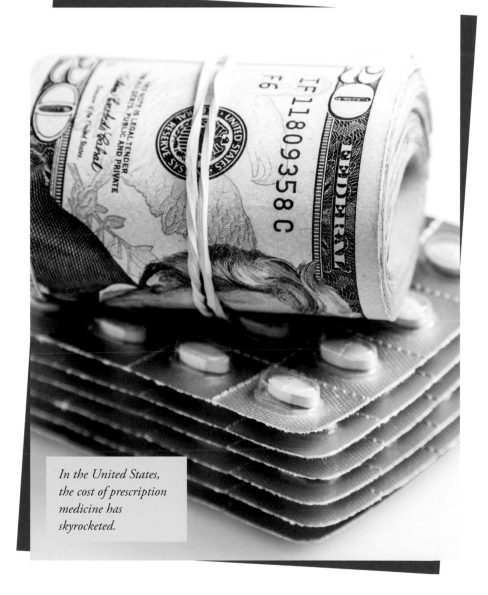

In the United States, the cost of prescription medicine has skyrocketed.

We Need to Lower Drug Prices

"Support for Medicare negotiations crumbles to just 31 percent when people are told that pharmaceutical companies may cut back on research if prices decline."

Alison Kodjak

In the following viewpoint, Alison Kodjak addresses the cost of prescription drugs in the United States. Many Americans struggle to pay for their medications. Even people with health insurance may struggle because some drugs may not be covered by insurance, while others may require the patient to pay part of the cost. At the time this viewpoint was written, some politicians were discussing ways to lower drug prices. One response would be to allow Medicare to negotiate with drug companies. Medicare is the federal health insurance program that covers people who are 65 or older, plus some younger people with disabilities. Drug companies claim that lower prices would interfere with their research and development. Alison Kodjak is a health policy correspondent for National Public Radio (NPR).

1. How many people believe drug prices are too high, according to the viewpoint?
2. How do drug companies spend their money?
3. What are some possible ways the government could help limit drug prices?

About a quarter of Americans surveyed say they've had trouble paying for their prescription drugs, and a majority welcome government action to help cut the cost of medications.

A survey released Friday by the nonpartisan Kaiser Family Foundation finds that many people have skipped or rationed their prescription medications or have substituted cheaper over-the-counter drugs.

The result? Those who ration their meds are often sicker, the poll finds.

The responses also illustrate why prescription drug prices are such a big issue for the Trump administration and on Capitol Hill.

"We've heard a lot of stories about the high prices that millions of American patients pay, and struggle to pay, for their drugs every month," Health and Human Services secretary Alex Azar said in a speech to the Bipartisan Policy Center on Feb. 1.

Azar was touting one of a series of regulatory proposals that he says will bring down prescription drug prices for consumers.

The survey suggests that a change like that would be well received. Seventy-nine percent of respondents said drug prices are unreasonable. And 63 percent said there's not as much regulation as there should be to help limit the price of prescription drugs.

"Financial barriers for medication use are not rare, and they can actually have and are having a detrimental effect on our fellow citizens' health," Inmaculada Hernandez, a professor at the University of Pittsburgh School of Pharmacy, said in an email. "With the current awareness and the bipartisan agreement in the recognition of drug prices as a major concern, we are in an optimal environment for the design and implementation of policies targeted at controlling prices, and assuring the affordability of medications to the US public."

In 2019, executives from the world's largest drug companies testified before Congress.

The poll also offers some guidance about which proposals would be most popular and which arguments proponents and opponents would be able to use to sway public opinion their way.

For example, 86 percent of respondents say they support having Medicare negotiate directly with drug companies to get lower prices.

Right now, Medicare is barred from direct negotiations, but Rep. Lloyd Doggett, D-Texas, and Sen. Sherrod Brown, D-Ohio, introduced a bill last month that would change that—a move drug companies oppose.

The poll shows that consumer support grows when people are told that such a change could lead to lower prices for senior citizens.

But that support for Medicare negotiations crumbles to just 31 percent when people are told that pharmaceutical companies may cut back on research if prices decline.

Richard Gonzalez, CEO of drugmaker AbbVie, said just that at a Senate Finance Committee hearing on Tuesday. In response to a question, he said AbbVie makes a profit in European countries, where its prices are much lower.

But if US prices fell to the same level, he warned, "I can just tell you that AbbVie would not be able to invest in the level of R&D that it invests in today." AbbVie makes the biologic drug Humira, which is the bestselling prescription drug in the world.

It's unclear that this argument will hold up, as the debate over the drug-negotiation bill in Congress progresses. Sen. Debbie Stabenow, D-Mich., responded by saying that the pharmaceutical industry spent $79 billion on sales, marketing and administration last year—$22 billion more than it spent on research.

The poll finds that 80 percent of Americans surveyed say that drug company profits are a major factor contributing to the price of prescription drugs. And only 25 percent trust drugmakers to price their products fairly, the poll finds.

The poll also finds that 65 percent of people surveyed support tying the price that Medicare pays for prescription drugs to the prices paid by the health services of other countries.

The Department of Health and Human Services has proposed that the prices of some cancer, arthritis and other medications administered in doctors' offices and hospitals be based on an index of prices paid in other developed countries.

A group of 57 conservative organizations opposes the idea. "The proposed payment model imports foreign price controls into the US," the group warned in a letter to the department.

But the Kaiser poll finds that the 65 percent of people who like the idea is almost the same as the share who favor outright limits to Medicare recipients' out-of-pocket costs.

The survey also finds widespread support, 88 percent, for another Trump administration initiative—requiring drug companies to include their products' list prices in television, magazine and other direct-to-consumer ads.

The nationwide survey of 1,440 adults was conducted from Feb. 14 to 24. The margin of error for the poll overall is plus or minus 3 percentage points.

EVALUATING THE AUTHOR'S ARGUMENTS:

In this viewpoint, Alison Kodjak introduces some possible ways to lower the price of prescription drugs. Some groups expressed concern about tying US drug prices to prices in other developed countries, such as in Europe. What are the possible benefits of making sure US prices match prices in other countries? What are potential problems?

Proposals to Lower Drug Prices Are Risky

Jim Greenwood and David Beier

"Compulsory licensing and international reference pricing are counter-productive and antithetical to the best interests of patients."

In the following viewpoint, Jim Greenwood and David Beier discuss the price of prescription drugs. The authors go into more detail about some of the government proposals under discussion. They claim that some major proposals would have negative consequences. Instead of making medicines more affordable, these proposals might lead to fewer new drugs. Greenwood and Beier argue that the United States produces the greatest number of new medicines because the country's current policies support innovation. Jim Greenwood is president and CEO of the Biotechnology Innovation Organization. David Beier is managing director of a venture capital firm investing in life science companies.

AS YOU READ, CONSIDER THE FOLLOWING QUESTIONS:
1. What would happen if the US government negotiated drug prices under Medicare, according to the authors?
2. What are compulsory licensing and international reference pricing?
3. What percentage of drugs make it through clinical programs to test if they are safe and effective?

With a new Democratic majority in the House pledging to address the rising cost of health care—including prescription drugs—a fundamental question arises: Will lawmakers focus on the real issues that can drain a family's finances, or simply adopt extreme policies that fail to take on the underlying problems in our health care system?

As policy professionals from different sides of the aisle, we believe there is a right way to address these issues and a wrong way. The right way will reduce out-of-pocket costs for Americans, improve access to new medicines, and allow the United States to remain the global leader in medical innovation. The wrong way leads to price controls, weakened intellectual property protections, and restricted access to medicines, not to mention stifling innovation and doing little to make drugs more affordable.

Judging from the current state of the drug-pricing debate, we are concerned that policymakers will adopt the wrong approach.

Take Medicare, for example. Leading politicians are calling on the government to directly "negotiate" drug prices under Medicare's prescription drug program. But the Congressional Budget Office has concluded that this proposal won't lower prices *unless* the government also restricts access to new medical breakthroughs.

Denying patients access to the medicines they need has never been popular. One proposal would give Medicare the power to directly negotiate drug prices. When the government doesn't get the price its demands, federal bureaucrats would have the power to seize the drug developer's intellectual property rights and give them to their competitors.

It gets worse. Another proposal would void the intellectual property of any drug with a price that exceeds the artificially low price

Pharmaceutical companies claim that the high price tags for prescription drugs fund research and development.

controls set by foreign countries with socialized health care. This pricing scheme would apply to any medicine or treatment sold within the US health care system, not just those provided through Medicare.

These ideas, known as compulsory licensing and international reference pricing, are counterproductive and antithetical to the best interests of patients. They fail the key test that any drug pricing proposal should have to pass: Are people who suffer from disease better off?

The United States develops more new medicines than the rest of the world combined precisely because we reject government price controls and assaults on intellectual property. Instead, our policies provide incentives for biomedical discovery through temporary market protection for innovators followed by generic competition.

This social compact works for all Americans—boosting our innovation economy, accelerating access to innovative treatments, and creating the most robust marketplace for cheaper generic medicines in the developed world.

If we go down the path of government control, we will destroy the delicate balance between innovation and competition. It costs on average $2.6 billion for each drug that successfully makes it to market, and more than 90 percent of clinical programs for new drugs ultimately fail. Further, more than 70 percent of drug development programs are being led by small biotechnology companies, which rely heavily on private-sector investments over a decade or more.

If forced to confront price controls and compulsory licensing, investors will put their money in the latest gadget rather than the next miracle cure. And if America targets its own innovators for such treatment, we can be sure that other countries would eagerly do the same for their innovators. The result? The number of new cures and treatments would be cut dramatically, which is bad news for the tens of millions of people who currently lack effective treatments.

That is a heavy price to pay when there is little evidence that compulsory licensing actually works. Indeed, there is no guarantee that any company receiving such a license would sell its copycat product for less, or that any savings would flow to patients. And what hasn't been discussed is that when the government seizes property, it must pay reasonable compensation for it, creating a potentially significant liability for taxpayers.

The midterm election would be a missed opportunity if Congress fails to provide real relief to vulnerable patients and seniors. They and their families are too smart to accept a flawed bargain of potentially lower drug list prices in exchange for denial of robust access to the medicines they need today—and fewer new medicines tomorrow.

Rather than pursuing policies that will destroy innovation and harm patients, we need to adopt responsible reforms that make a meaningful difference in the lives of all patients by reducing their out-of-pocket expenses for prescription drugs and improving access to innovative medicines. There are numerous ideas available to help do just that, such as removing regulatory barriers to value-based pricing and capping what seniors must pay for medicines in Medicare.

We know what the right approach is for lowering prescription drug costs. All we need is for our elected policymakers to take it.

The Cost of Pharmaceutical Research and Development Is Increasing

Thomas Sullivan

"Drug development remains a costly undertaking despite ongoing efforts across the full spectrum of pharmaceutical and biotech companies to rein in growing R&D costs."

In the following viewpoint, Thomas Sullivan explores the cost of bringing a drug to market. The author examines a recent study that found that the expense of bringing a drug to market has increased drastically in the last decade. This study lists the current cost as $2.6 billion per new drug. Most drugs never make it to market. The expense of testing these medications is included when considering the cost of successful drugs. Some people have questioned the results of this study, arguing it did not include enough detail to be reliable. Thomas Sullivan is a former political consultant for Policy & Medicine, a daily news report on the pharmaceutical industry.

"A Tough Road: Cost to Develop One New Drug Is $2.6 Billion; Approval Rate for Drugs Entering Clinical Development Is Less Than 12%," by Thomas Sullivan, Policy & Medicine, March 21, 2019. Reprinted by permission.

AS YOU READ, CONSIDER THE FOLLOWING QUESTIONS:
  1. What percentage of drugs make it to market?
  2. What is to blame for the increasing costs of drug development, according to the viewpoint?
  3. Why were some people skeptical about the Tufts study?

Developing a new prescription medicine that gains marketing approval is estimated to cost drugmakers $2.6 billion according to a recent study by Tufts Center for the Study of Drug Development and published in the *Journal of Health Economics*. This is up from $802 million in 2003—equal to approximately $1 billion in 2013 dollars, and thus a 145 percent increase in the ten year study gap. Furthermore, while the average time it takes to bring a drug through clinical trials has decreased, the rate of success has gone down by almost half, to just 12 percent.

Tufts breaks down its $2.558 billion figure per approved compound to include approximate average out-of-pocket cost of $1.4 billion and time costs (the expected returns that investors forego while a drug is in development) of $1.2 billion.

Furthermore, the estimated cost of post-approval research and development of $312 million "boosts the full product lifecycle cost per approved drug" to close to $3 billion. R&D costs include studies to test new indications, new formulations, new dosage strength and regimens, and to monitor safety and long-term side effects in patients, as required by the FDA as a condition of approval.

Tufts' analysis was developed from information provided by 10 pharmaceutical companies on 106 randomly selected drugs that were first tested in human subjects anywhere in the world from 1995 to 2007.

"Drug development remains a costly undertaking despite ongoing efforts across the full spectrum of pharmaceutical and biotech companies to rein in growing R&D costs," stated Joseph A. DiMasi, director of economic analysis at Tufts CSDD and principal investigator for the study. "Because the R&D process is marked by substantial technical risks, with expenditures incurred for many development projects that fail to result in a marketed product, our estimate links

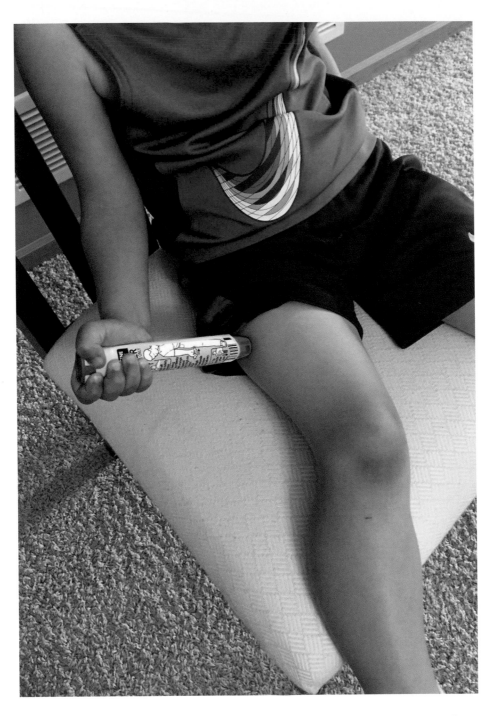

In 2016, the price of the EpiPen, which is used to combat severe allergic reactions, soared from $100 to $600 for a pack of two. Public outrage forced the company that makes it to offer a more affordable generic option.

the costs of unsuccessful projects to those that are successful in obtaining marketing approval from regulatory authorities."

According to DiMasi, rising drug development costs have been driven mainly by increases in out-of-pocket costs for individual drugs and higher failure rates for drugs tested in human subjects. This explanation stuck out to Don Seiffert, editor of BioFlash, who listened to DiMasi's presentation last week: "Based on an analysis of 1,442 experimental drugs that were in clinical tests in recent years through the end of 2013, DiMasi said the overall chance that a drug entering clinical development will be approved for marketing is just under 12 percent."

"Approximately seven out of eight compounds that enter the clinical testing pipeline will fail in development," DiMasi said. "Put another way, you need to put an average of 8.5 compounds in clinical development to get one approval."

Seiffert notes that DiMasi arrived at the 12 percent figure using a "weighted average, since as of the study, just 7 percent of the 1,442 drugs had actually been approved. Fully 80 percent had been abandoned by the companies developing them, and the other 13 percent were still in active development. DiMasi said it's likely that many of the drugs in later development will eventually earn approval, hence the overall 12 percent rate."

The previous study set a success rate for drugs that enter human trials at 21.5 percent.

According to DiMasi, factors that likely have boosted out-of-pocket clinical costs include increased clinical trial complexity, larger clinical trial sizes, higher cost of inputs from the medical sector used for development, greater focus on targeting chronic and degenerative diseases, changes in protocol design to include efforts to gather health technology assessment information, and testing on comparator drugs to accommodate payer demands for comparative effectiveness data.

Consumer Advocate Groups Scrutinize Study

After the Tufts press release, a number of consumer advocates and academics took various shots at the data. James Love of Knowledge Ecology International believes the study is "long on propaganda, and short of details." Love urges readers to "put some pressure on Tufts to provide more details of what the data looks like." He references the most recent industry funded study on drug costs, from 2012, entitled "The R&D Cost of a New Medicine," published in the Office of Health Economics (OHE). That study found R&D cost to be $1.506 billion. "[That] report was 98 pages," he states. "So far, we have a press release of 579 words" from Tufts.

Love questions a number of aspects of the study, including the fact that the study assumes that NIH provided no funding in the pre-clinical development of drugs. Furthermore, Love states that "we don't know how many patients were in the trials (that were used to calculate the estimate) or how much money was claimed to have been spent per patient in the trials. Since the entire estimate was based upon the costs of the trials, we don't have any idea of what the sample looked like."

DiMasi responded to some of these critiques in the *Wall Street Journal*:

> [T]he OHE analysis was based on a small sample (with regard to clinical testing) of projects that were in some phase of clinical development from 1997 to 1999 and followed only to 2002. The data for our study are effectively much more recent than the data used for the OHE report.
>
> What we are measuring is what private developers actually spent on development. NIH research is complementary. If the NIH does some basic research, or even clinical research, that has findings that developers find interesting and useful, then the cost of that NIH research is just part of the social cost of drug development.

The social cost is the private cost PLUS what governments and non-profits spend that somehow contributes to the discovery and development of new drugs. If private developers spend less than they otherwise would because of the NIH research, then that is captured in our estimate because we are only measuring what private developers spent.

EVALUATING THE AUTHOR'S ARGUMENTS:

Viewpoint author Thomas Sullivan shows that calculating the cost of a new drug is complicated. Studies may be conducted in different ways and come up with different results. How can the resulting statistics be used to promote certain viewpoints?

Drug Research Isn't as Costly as Companies Claim

Donald W. Light and Hagop Kantarjian

"Oncologists find that most new cancer drugs provide few clinical advantages over existing ones."

In the following viewpoint, Donald W. Light and Hagop Kantarjian look at the cost of cancer treatments. The authors argue against the claims that high research and development costs lead to better treatments. They note that newer cancer drugs offer little, if any, benefit over previous drugs. Yet they are much more expensive. The authors then argue that drug companies calculate the cost in a misleading way. The actual cost may be far lower than other sources claim. Donald W. Light is a professor of comparative health at Rowan University in New Jersey. Hagop Kantarjian, M.D., is an oncologist and the chair of the Leukemia Department at MD Anderson Cancer Center.

"Cancer Drugs' Rising Costs: The $100,000 Myth," by Donald W. Light and Hagop Kantarjian, American Association of Retired Persons (AARP). Reprinted by permission.

E very patient with cancer wants the most effective treatment, but drug prices have become staggering. Eleven of the 12 new cancer drugs approved in 2012 were priced above $100,000 annually, and a 20 to 30 percent copayment can make them unaffordable even for well-insured patients.

Why are companies charging so much? In one breath they say high prices reflect high research costs, and in the next they say prices reflect the precious added benefits of curing or controlling cancer. We find neither explanation plausible.

The argument that companies are offering improved drugs for these higher prices is not true. Oncologists find that most new cancer drugs provide few clinical advantages over existing ones. Only one of the 12 new cancer drugs approved in 2012 helps patients survive more than two months longer.

The industry argument that high prices reflect huge research and development costs also does not hold up, at least given the few facts that companies make public to back it up. Indeed, the actual dollars that companies have put into research from 1995 to 2010 have generated six times more revenue—a sign that they are charging too much for little patient benefit.

Inflated Costs

The most famous industry-sponsored estimate claims that it costs on average $1.3 billion to develop a new drug and get it approved. This includes the cost of failures. Half that estimate, however, is not research cost at all, but rather a high figure for profits that companies would have made if they had invested their research money in

Many consumers are fed up with what they perceive to be greed on the part of "big pharma" companies. The justifications for high drug prices don't always seem true.

stocks and bonds instead. Profits forgone is a common way of estimating whether it's worthwhile to undertake a new project. But it is not a real cost that must be recouped from customers. Eliminating it brings the actual research costs down from $1.3 billion to $650 million.

In addition, taxpayers subsidize about half of company research costs through credits and deductions granted to drug companies. This brings companies' real research costs down to $325 million.

Moreover, the industry's $1.3 billion is based on a sample of the most costly fifth of new drugs, not the average for all drugs. Correcting this distortion brings company research costs down by 30 percent, to $230 million. Also, a few expensive projects always inflate the overall average, so it's more accurate to use the median cost—the point at which half of the research projects cost more and half less. This brings company research costs down to $170 million. Further, clinical trials in cancer are smaller and shorter than trials for other diseases, so trial costs should be smaller, too.

A final way in which research costs are inflated is by backing in a large estimate for the cost of basic research to discover new drugs.

In fact, no accurate estimate exists because the costs of discovery vary so much, from an inexpensive lucky break to a costly 30-year search before a new drug is discovered. Removing that inflated estimate for basic research costs brings the net, median corporate research costs down to just $125 million for developing drugs.

The Price Push

Overall, investment in basic research by pharmaceutical companies to discover new drugs is quite small—about one-sixth of overall company research costs and about 1.3 percent of revenues after deducting for taxpayer subsidies. The rest of company research costs goes to developing all these drugs with few advantages over existing ones so they can charge high prices for them.

In the case of cancer drugs, company research costs are even lower, because most of the basic research and thousands of clinical trials are paid for by the National Cancer Institute and foundations.

In sum, we find no credible evidence that the real research costs to major companies themselves for cancer research are higher than for developing other drugs. So why are cancer drug prices higher? We think pharmaceutical companies are price-gouging. Even worse, companies raise the prices on some of their older drugs by 20 to 25 percent a year. In the past decade, they have almost doubled their prices for cancer drugs.

We call this the "market spiral pricing strategy"—continually raising prices across the whole market, regardless of value or cost. No other advanced country allows companies to raise prices on older drugs. No other industry raises prices on last year's cars or cellphones.

Congress should hold hearings on the spiraling prices for specialty drugs. And it should eliminate the rule that prohibits Medicare from negotiating discount drug prices. Then physicians could treat patients with drugs they can afford. These changes could substantially cut the nation's health care costs and provide incentives for companies to focus on developing clinically better drugs rather than slightly better drugs at sky-high prices.

EVALUATING THE AUTHORS' ARGUMENTS:

Review Viewpoints 2, 3, and 4 in this chapter. Which one seems to have the most accurate information about the cost of bringing new drugs to market? Why did you make that choice? Does the author or publication influence your opinion? With this new information, go back to Viewpoint 1. How do those government proposals sound now?

Government Regulation Drives Up Drug Prices for Patients

Laura Williams and Dan Sanchez

"By stifling competition, regulation can protect the market share of the big boys at the expense of patients."

In the following viewpoint, Laura Williams and Dan Sanchez argue that the US government plays a part in the rising costs of drug prices in the country. The authors explain that aggressive government regulation of medications creates a system that restricts supply and competition, two essential aspects of creating affordable goods in a free market. The result is that patients are forced to pay sky-high prices or forgo medication altogether, while big pharma CEOs and government bureaucrats only get richer. Dr. Laura Williams teaches communication strategy to undergraduates and executives. Dan Sanchez is the director of content at the Foundation for Economic Education (FEE) and the editor of FEE.org.

AS YOU READ, CONSIDER THE FOLLOWING QUESTIONS:
1. What does Elizabeth Warren leave out of her argument about corruption, according to the authors?
2. Why is insulin so expensive if the treatment itself is relatively cheap?
3. What is "regulatory capture" and how does it benefit big drug companies?

What does it take to get vital medical care in America? For Laura Matson, a type-1 diabetic, it took upending her whole life. To pay for her insulin treatments, she had to sell her car and furniture, relocate, and even give away her dog Nicky, as the BBC reported. And she is not alone. Many Americans struggle to make ends meet as their health care costs rise.

These rising costs are strange, in a sense. The prices of other consumer goods—nutritious food, digital devices, clothing, etc.—generally fall as technology advances and production becomes more efficient. Why is health care such an exception to this rule?

After all, most of the medications Americans take are made of relatively simple ingredients. And once treatments are established, drugs cost very little to produce. Insulin itself is a century-old technology. So why are Ms. Matson's insulin treatments so expensive?

Senator Elizabeth Warren blames corruption. At a recent Democratic debate, Warren said:

> *Who is this economy really working for? It's doing great for a thinner and thinner slice at the top. It's doing great for giant drug companies. It's just not doing great for people who need a prescription filled…*
>
> *When you've got a government, when you've got an economy that does great for those with money and isn't doing great for everyone else, that is corruption, pure and simple. We need to call it out. We need to attack it head on. And we need to make structural change in our government, in our economy, and in our country.*

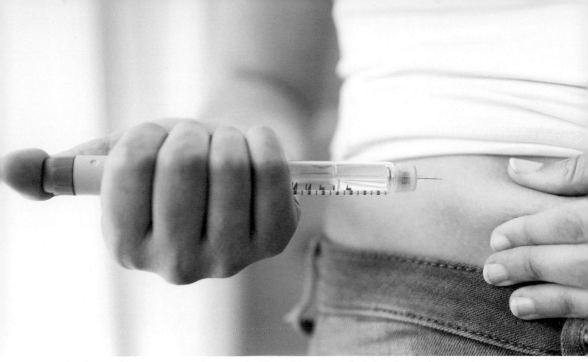

Diabetes is becoming an epidemic in the United States, so why is insulin used to treat it so expensive? Many patients can't afford to pay for the treatments they need to manage the disease.

To an extent, Warren is right: corruption is the problem. The pharma-to-patient pipeline is clogged with it. What she leaves out is the key role that government regulation plays in that corruption.

How Regulation Makes Health Care More Expensive

Regulation in the health care industry drives up prices for patients in many ways.

The Food and Drug Administration's approval system requires billions of dollars and nearly a decade to navigate. This strangles supply by hampering production and constrains competition by preventing smaller companies from entering the market. And as Econ 101 informs us, lower supply and less competition mean higher prices.

Federal patent policy also restricts supply and competition, especially by blocking generics. For example, as one of us wrote earlier this year in "A Government Guide to Keeping Insulin Unaffordable: 3 Easy Steps to Hogtie a Market":

> *Even though insulin treatment itself can't be patented, improvements in delivery mechanisms can be. These*

incremental improvements, no matter how small, can be used to extend the 20-year patent on a drug, a process called "patent evergreening." Sanofi has filed 74 patent applications on its long-acting insulin Lantus—nearly all of them after the drug was on the market—and boxed out generics for decades. Drug makers seek extensions to their exclusivity when they add pill coatings and alter inactive ingredients, extending their monopoly but offering no marginal advantage to patients.

Cheaper drugs of comparable quality produced abroad are simply illegal to import or resell in the US.

At every stage where regulation narrows the choices available, patients lose. Life-saving treatments become harder to access and more expensive.

To return to Laura Matson, regulation drove up the cost of her insulin treatments by limiting competitive market innovation at every opportunity. A generic version of a drug or insulin injector pump can drop the price by up to 90 percent, but the government blocks generics. Nearly identical, perfectly safe insulin products can be bought from Canadian drug makers, but imports are illegal. Heavily regulated insurance issuers are legally limited to a handful in each state, and each plan reimburses only some brands.

Pharmacies could dispense treatments popular in the 1990s for pennies, instead of the expensive, cutting-edge tech. Ms. Matson might have been willing to test her blood sugar more than once a day with tedious strips or deal with the hassle of vials and needles if it meant she could keep her apartment and her beloved dog. But regulations deny her that choice.

Patients Lose—So Who Wins?

If you want to understand any regulatory scheme, ask yourself, who benefits from it? Policymakers may have pitched the rules as protections for patients—indeed that may have been the sincere intention of some. But clearly, the system does not benefit Ms. Matson or others like her. When a dirt-cheap, exceptionally common prescription like insulin keeps getting more costly while everything less regulated becomes less expensive, the regulations are standing in the way of progress.

So if not patients, who benefits?

The executives and shareholders of big, established pharmaceutical companies certainly do. They hold the valuable patents that prevent generics competitors from underselling them. And FDA compliance costs may hurt their bottom line, but they are big enough to absorb them, while smaller would-be competitors are not. So regulation creates a barrier to entry—a "you must be this big to ride" bar—that keeps out upstart competitors.

By stifling competition in the above ways, regulation can protect the market share of the big boys, granting them inflated, cushy profit margins, at the expense of patients, who pay inflated, onerous prices for care.

Of course, FDA bureaucrats benefit, too: a lengthy approval process provides them highly paid jobs. And for many of them, the gravy train doesn't stop there. Big pharmaceutical companies often hire former regulators at very generous salaries to help navigate the FDA gauntlet.

Scott Gottlieb was FDA commissioner until just months ago and is now on Pfizer Inc.'s Board of Directors. Current Secretary of Health and Human Services Alex Azar is a former Eli Lilly executive.

A revolving door between regulatory agencies and the companies they're regulating creates pressure to be "good for (big) business." Doing little favors for one another (downplaying an unfavorable trial, tying a competitor up in some extra red tape, delaying the approval of a generic alternative) overrides public interest as former and future colleagues play a slow, highly profitable game of musical chairs.

The Problem of Regulatory Capture

When regulatory agencies are thus "captured" by big players in the industries they regulate, it is called "regulatory capture." Regulatory capture runs rampant in highly regulated industries, and it is not too hard to understand why.

In a free market, the way to "win the game" is straightforward and fixed: serve your customers better than your competitors do. But in a highly regulated market, the rules of the game are malleable. This opens a new path to success: helping to make regulations that disadvantage your competitors.

Influencing the rules of the game then becomes a big part of the game. Instead of playing better, you can win by calling the referee and getting your opponent thrown out. So gaining sway over the rule-makers and rule-enforcers (regulators) becomes paramount, and satisfying customers less so.

FAST FACT

Pharmaceutical companies spend $19 on advertising a new drug for every one dollar spent on research and development. It takes approximately 10 to 15 years for drugs approved by the US FDA to get through testing and reach patients.

The free-market "satisfy the customer" game has historically been characterized by businesses rising and falling. Time after time, incumbent Goliaths are brought down by upstart Davids. (Think of Netflix busting Blockbuster.) Out of the companies in the Fortune 500 of 1955, only 52 still ranked on that list in 2019.

But in the regulated-market "cripple your competitor" game, the Goliaths have an extra advantage. With their lobbying budgets and political connections, they are in a better position to capture their regulators and rig the rules of the game in their favor.

Regulatory Power Corrupts

So Senator Warren is right in a sense: prescription drugs are indeed expensive because of corruption. But that corruption is made possible (and irresistible) by regulation. Power corrupts, and regulatory power is no exception. This is not a problem of capitalism, but of cronyism: a symbiotic relationship between big government and big business.

And Warren's proposed solutions—further concentrating power with a Medicare for All plan, or letting government agencies oversee production of generic drugs—would only make the problem worse. Imagine the profitability of requiring only name-brand drugs through Medicare; giving regulators more power increases interest groups' incentives to manipulate regulators instead of serving customers.

The real solution to rising health care costs is less regulatory power, not more. The great disruptors that lower prices and accelerate access—the Amazons and AirBnBs of health care—are out there, but regulation is standing in their way. As long as regulators have the power to exclude products and companies from the marketplace, some businesses will try to game the system instead of upping their game. Less rule-rigging would mean more competition, more services, and lower prices for people like Laura Matson.

EVALUATING THE AUTHORS' ARGUMENTS:

In the viewpoint, authors Laura Williams and Dan Sanchez argue that government regulation is to blame for high drug costs. If this is true, how can the government ensure medical treatment is both safe and affordable? How does this viewpoint fit with other arguments for lowering drug prices?

Educate the Public to Lower Drug Costs

> *"The United States also pays significantly higher prices than the rest of the developed world when it comes to prescription drugs."*

Simon F. Haeder

In the following viewpoint, Simon F. Haeder notes that Americans spend more per year on prescription medicine than Europeans. He mentions several causes but puts most of the blame on pharmaceutical companies trying to get the highest profits. The author argues that the Trump administration's proposal to lower drug costs has some drawbacks. A better plan would address the underlying market dynamics. Germany evaluates the benefit provided by a new drug after it is released. This information is used to negotiate the price between drug manufacturers and health plans. Perhaps something similar would work in the United States. Simon F. Haeder is an assistant professor in the Department of Political Science at West Virginia University.

AS YOU READ, CONSIDER THE FOLLOWING QUESTIONS:
1. For how long has the US been the biggest spender when it comes to drug costs?
2. How does drug advertising in the US compare to Europe?
3. How would costs shift between consumers if the Trump administration's plan passes, according to the viewpoint?

S pending on pharmaceuticals is on the rise worldwide. And it well should be. Today, we are able to cure some diseases like hepatitis C that were virtual death sentences just a few years ago. This progress required significant investments by governments and private companies alike. Unquestionably, the world is better off for it.

Unfortunately, as President Trump pointed out in the State of the Union address, the United States has borne a significant amount of the negative effects associated with this development. For one, its regulatory apparatus has focused largely on drug safety, yet regulators have failed to emphasize cost-effectiveness when it comes to both new and existing drugs.

At the same time, the United States also pays significantly higher prices than the rest of the developed world when it comes to prescription drugs, due primarily to limited competition among drug companies.

These two problems are well-known to policymakers, consumers and scholars alike. The Trump administration's recent proposal seeks to lower costs by restructuring drug discounts that occur between pharmaceutical companies, health insurers and entities called pharmacy benefit managers.

But in my view as a health policy scholar, the plan does little to address the underlying problems of prescription drugs in the US. I believe the US can refocus its regulatory approach to pharmaceuticals, adapted from the one used in Europe, to better connect the value prescription drugs provide and their price.

The US and Other Countries

Until the mid-1990s, the US was really not an outlier when it came to drug spending. Countries like Germany and France exceeded

There are several reasons why we are spending more at the pharmacy than we used to.

the US in per capita drug spending. However, since then, spending growth in the US has dramatically outpaced other advanced nations. While per capita spending in the US today exceeds US$1,000 a year, the Germans and French pay about half that.

And it is not like Americans are overly reliant on prescription drugs as compared to their European counterparts. Americans use fewer prescription drugs, and when they use them, they are more likely to use cheaper generic versions. Instead the discrepancy can be traced back to the issue plaguing the entirety of the US health care system: prices.

The reasons for the divergence starting in the 1990s are relatively straightforward. For one, dozens of so-called blockbuster drugs like Lipitor and Advair entered the market. The number of drugs grossing more than $1 billion in sales increased from six in 1997 to 52 in 2006. The recent introduction of extremely pricey drugs treating hepatitis C are only the latest of these.

Lacking even rudimentary price controls, US consumers bore the full brunt of the expensive development work that goes into new drugs. These costs were further augmented by marketing expenditures and profit seeking by all entities within the

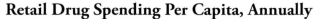

Retail Drug Spending Per Capita, Annually

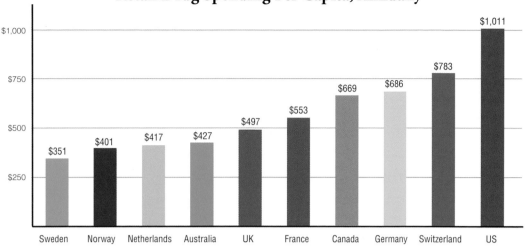

Sweden	Norway	Netherlands	Australia	UK	France	Canada	Germany	Switzerland	US
$351	$401	$417	$427	$497	$553	$669	$686	$783	$1,011

Source: The Commonwealth Fund

Compared to the rest of the world, Americans spend the most on drugs, by far.

pharmaceutical supply chain. Consumers in Europe, where there are government-controlled checks on prices, were not as exposed to those high costs.

The Food and Drug Administration has also consistently moved to relax direct-to-consumer advertising regulations, a practice that is either banned or severely limited in most other advanced nations. While there are limited information benefits to consumers, this practice has certainly increased consumption of high-priced drugs.

Additionally, the overall complexity of the US health care system and the lack of transparency in the drug supply chain system create conditions favorable to limited competition and price maximization.

All entities in the pharmaceutical supply chain, including manufacturers and wholesale distributors, have become extremely skilled at finding regulatory loopholes that allow them to maximize profits. This includes, for example, creatively expanding the life of patents, or having them recategorized as "orphan drugs" for rare disease to preserve monopolies. So-called pharmacy benefit managers, the middlemen that administer prescription drug programs, add further complexity and often may be driven by profit maximization.

Finally, the US has undergone a series of coverage expansions, including the prominent creation of the Children's Health Insurance Program, Medicare Part D, and the Affordable Care Act. For many of the newly covered, this meant access to prescription drugs for the first time and pent-up demand was released. However, it also encouraged pharmaceutical companies to take advantage of the newfound payers for their drugs.

Trump's Proposed Fixes

The consequences of pricey pharmaceuticals are significant in terms of costs and diminished health. Close to 20 percent of adults report skipping medications because they are concerned about costs. Nonetheless, the US may be spending close to $500 billion annually.

The plan proposed by the Trump administration basically replaces an opaque discount arrangement between drug makers, insurers and middlemen called pharmacy benefit managers with a discount program directly aimed at consumers. Particularly benefiting from the change would be those individuals requiring costly non-generic drugs. Unquestionably, their lives would improve due to increased access and lower costs.

At the same time, costs would be shifted to healthier consumers who do not rely on expensive drugs, as well as those relying on generic versions. Both will be faced with higher overall insurance premiums while not seeing any reductions in the prescription drug bills. That's because insurers would no longer be able to use drug discounts to hold down premiums.

The Trump administration's discounting approach, however, is not uncommon. The Veterans Health Administration's has done so quite successfully, obtaining discounts in the range of 40 percent. Likewise, Medicaid programs are also using their purchasing power to obtain discounts. And calls for Medicare to negotiate discounts with pharmaceutical companies are common.

The way I see it, there are three major issues inherent in negotiating discounts for drugs.

For one, true negotiations would only take place if Medicare or any other entity was willing to walk away from certain drugs if no discounts could be obtained. In a country that heavily values choice, and where such activities would become a political football, this is highly unlikely.

Moreover, it would only work for drugs where viable alternatives are available. After all, most Americans would likely be hesitant to exclude a drug, even at high costs, when no alternative cure exists.

Yet even if some version of a discount program were to be implemented more widely, such a program does not change the underlying pricing or market dynamics. Crucially, relying on discounts does nothing to reduce list prices set by manufacturers. Pharmaceutical companies and all other entities in the supply chain remain free to set prices, bring products to the market, and take advantage of loopholes to maximize corporate profits.

Ultimately, pharmaceutical companies and all other entities involved in the pharmaceutical supply chain are unlikely to be willing to simply give up profits. Quite likely, steeper discounts for Medicaid and Medicare may lead to higher costs for employer-sponsored plans.

Focusing on Effectiveness and Consumer Information

The question then emerges: What could be done to truly improve the twin issues of high costs and limited cost-effectiveness when comes to pharmaceuticals in the US health care system?

While Americans are often hesitant to learn from other countries, looking to Europe when it comes to pharmaceuticals holds much promise. Countries like Britain and Germany have taken extensive steps to introduce assessments of cost-effectiveness into their health care systems, refusing to pay higher prices for new drugs that do not improve effectiveness of treatment over existing options.

Since reforming its system in the early 2010s, Germany has allowed manufacturers to freely set prices for a limited period when bringing new drugs to the market. It then uses the data available from that period for a nongovernmental and nonprofit research body to evaluate the benefit provided by the new drug, as compared to existing alternatives. This added benefit, or lack thereof, then serves as the foundation for price negotiations between drug manufacturers and health plans.

While the legal restrictions and the fragmented nature of the US health care system severely limit the ability of the US to fully translate such a model, in my opinion, the underlying approach bears great value.

Lacking the corporatist nature of the Germany economy, the US should resort to a bottom-up approach focused on investing in assessing and subsequent publicizing of cost-effectiveness data as well as cost-benefit analyses for all drugs. In order to minimize politicization, these analyses would be best handled by one or multiple independent research institutes.

Ultimately, knowing what drugs provide what value would equally benefit consumers, providers, and payers, and serve as a meaningful first step towards connecting the prices we pay for prescriptions to the value we derive from them.

EVALUATING THE AUTHOR'S ARGUMENTS:

In this viewpoint, author Simon F. Haeder recommends publicizing how effective each drug is. The cost-benefit analysis, which analyzes the strengths and weaknesses of a treatment, would also be publicized. Do you think public access to this knowledge would help lower the cost of drugs? Why or why not?

Chapter 3

How Do Legal Drugs Contribute to Health Problems?

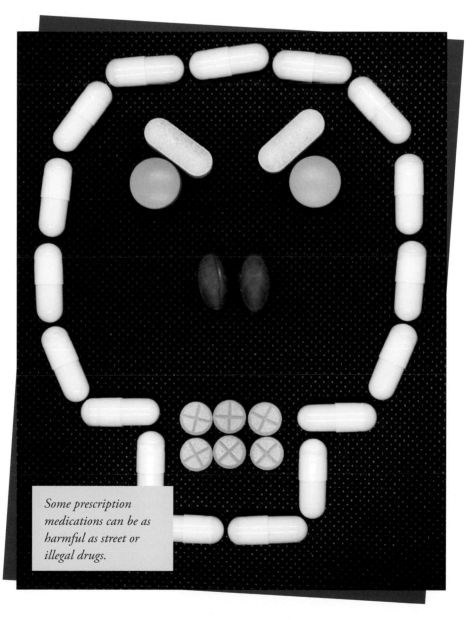

Some prescription medications can be as harmful as street or illegal drugs.

Viewpoint

1

Antidepressants Can Do More Harm Than Good

"Psychiatric medications, and specifically antidepressants are the most habit forming chemicals on the planet."

Kelly Brogan, M.D.

In the following viewpoint, Dr. Kelly Brogan describes a patient who suffered after discontinuing use of Zoloft, a medicine taken for depression, anxiety, and similar concerns. The author notes that stopping psychiatric medications can lead to serious withdrawal symptoms. Some doctors take this as a sign that patients should stay on the medicines forever. This author argues that there are better methods of treating mental illness. Dr. Kelly Brogan is a holistic psychiatrist and author of *A Mind of Your Own*, a book that looks at ways to heal depression without prescription medication.

AS YOU READ, CONSIDER THE FOLLOWING QUESTIONS:
1. How do psychiatric medicines compare to illegal drugs in terms of the potential for addiction?
2. How can antidepressants create imbalances, and what is the effect?
3. What physical and emotional elements can contribute to mental illness, according to the viewpoint?

"Letter to the New York Times: Many People Taking Antidepressants Discover They Can't Quit," by Dr. Kelly Brogan, M.D. Reprinted by permission.

Searing stomach pain, racing heart, hair loss, missed periods, flared psoriasis, burning fingers, constipation, confusion, frequent upper respiratory infections, and 9 months of intractable insomnia.

No, this is not why Rachel went on Zoloft in the first place. No this is not a "relapse." She came to me at the end of her rope, hanging on for dear life, at a point of desperation that she had never known possible when she filled that prescription 6 years ago after a breakup left her heartbroken. Now 4 months from her last dose, Rachel could spend the rest of her days visiting specialists and garnering new diagnoses chasing the elusive thread that links them all: psychiatric medication withdrawal.

I was trained to tell patients like Rachel that this is evidence they should remain on medication. I was taught to tell her that the medication was long out of her system given its "half life" and that these symptoms were unrelated to the fact that she stopped taking her Zoloft, and her distress around her condition, evidence that she should restart it.

Ten years ago, the recent *New York Times* article entitled *Many People Taking Antidepressants Discover They Can't Quit* would have shocked me. I would have dismissed serious medication withdrawal as rare if I acknowledged it at all.

But with ten years of experience in the wild unknown of psychiatric medication tapers, I tell my patients something different today. And I have accumulating scientific evidence to support my message about the seriousness of discontinuation.

In the first systematized review of SSRI withdrawal,[1] Fava et al. examined 23 studies and 38 case reports leading them to conclude that the euphemistic term "discontinuation syndrome" must be abandoned in lieu of a more accurate depiction of the habit-forming qualities of antidepressants—withdrawal. Yes, just like Xanax, Valium, alcohol, and heroin.

Relatedly, Chouinard and Chouinard state: "Patients can experience classic new withdrawal symptoms, rebound and/or persistent post-withdrawal disorders, or relapse/recurrence of the original illness. New and rebound symptoms can occur for up to 6 weeks after drug withdrawal, depending on the drug elimination half-life,

Prescription medications have helped many people who suffer from depression, but they also can be addictive.

while persistent post-withdrawal or tardive disorders associated with long-lasting receptor changes may persist for more than 6 weeks after drug discontinuation."[2]

They even provide a handy chart of the horrors that can befall unsuspecting patients ranging from those who miss a dosage to those who taper carefully.

How could this be happening? Medications aren't addictive! They're therapeutic. In an interesting twist in the history of allopathy, an inconvenient truth is emerging: we have a nation overrun by drug dealers. Only today's most lethal and disabling drug dealers have advanced degrees and Walter White-level biochemical acumen. Today, urban lyrics are replete with the tales of trafficked pharmaceuticals, artists are raging at their prescribers, and the opioid epidemic is impacting everyone from CEOs to grandmothers.

Sure, Xanax and oxycontin are addictive, but Prozac?

I have stated and will again, that psychiatric medications, and specifically antidepressants are the most habit forming chemicals on the planet. I've seen patients who have been disabled by a Celexa taper progressing at 0.001mg per month. I challenge you to find me comparable instances of crack cocaine, heroin, alcohol, or others meds that demand this level of care and caution to simply come off them.

In order to wrap our minds around this possibility, we have to first disabuse ourselves of the assumption that anti-depressants are "fixing" anything biochemically. They are not correcting an imbalance, a genetic defect, or healing the brain.

As Dr. Joanna Moncrieff has stated, antidepressants create imbalances.[3] One that the body then adapts to, and one that specifically recruits the stress response system, one possible explanation for how and why withdrawal from these medications set off alarm bells that reveal every weakened link in your physiology.

Andrews et al. have detailed the propensity of these medications to induce withdrawal, a phenomenon that relates not to the patient's clinical history, but to the chemical profile of the drug.[4]

Unfortunately, we also know that it can take longer than 17 years for basic science research that challenges consensus practice to trickle into the hands of the average clinician.[5]

So, now that we know this, why would someone even consider tapering? Why not just leave well enough alone?

Because medication is not a long-term solution. For some, it's not a solution at all, as evidenced by placebo-level efficacy[6] attended by an extreme list of unintended effects ranging from gastrointestinal hemorrhage to impulsive homicide.

All of the long-term naturalistic data available cautions that those who are treated with psychiatric medication for longer than two months function more poorly than those who were never treated. In fact, it was the long-term data reviewed in Robert Whitaker's book, *Anatomy of an Epidemic* that made me put down my prescription pad forever.[7]

Since that time, I have been supporting patient transitions to medication-free living and have outcomes including those published in the peer-reviewed literature[8, 9] that defy the dogmatic presumptions around mental illness as a chronic medical condition.

These individuals come off of medication and come alive in a new way.

How?

They dare to ask WHY. Why were they symptomatic to begin with? What was really beneath their diagnosis, sometimes made after a ten minute visit with a college health center doc. We move through a process of self-healing and personal reclamation that triages imbalances.

First we heal the physical body and address gut-brain inflammation, a well-recognized driver of psychiatric pathology. Through this process of a month-long lifestyle change protocol online and detailed in *A Mind of Your Own*, we address many reversible drivers of symptoms ranging from panic attacks to fatigue to obsessive compulsions. These drivers include blood sugar imbalance, food-based autoimmunity, nutrient deficiencies, and medication-driven effects including common meds like antibiotics and birth control pills.

Then we take an emotional inventory of the relationships and elements of one's life that are simply no longer working. With the renewed energy now reclaimed from the white noise of physical imbalances, these patients are ready to begin addressing what they may not have felt capable of turning toward in their life earlier—a toxic marriage, an oppressive job, a lack of community.

Invariably, there is an emergence of the deeper spiritual elements of healing that these med-free seekers encounter. They begin to explore the big questions: What am I here for? How can I give back? And the deeper why of their conditioned and patterned behavior—their childhood experiences and traumas.

Through this process, they become whole. And they understand that, as Rumi says, the wound is the place where the Light enters, and that we must make room for sadness, grief, and pain, in order to expand our capacity for joy and fulfillment.

As these survivors exit the birth canal of their tapering experience, the most common sentiment I am reported is: I finally feel like myself. Who knew that this was all we ever wanted.

Endnotes

1. http://www.karger.com/Article/FullText/370338

2. http://www.karger.com/Article/FullText/371865

3. http://journals.plos.org/plosmedicine/article?id=10.1371/journal.pmed.0030240

4. https://www.ncbi.nlm.nih.gov/pubmed/21779273

5. http://journals.sagepub.com/doi/abs/10.1258/jrsm.2011.110180

6. http://psycnet.apa.org/index.cfm?fa=buy.optionToBuy&id=1999-11094-001

7. http://www.power2u.org/downloads/AnatomyofanEpidemic-SummaryofFindings-Whitaker
.pdf

8. https://www.ncbi.nlm.nih.gov/pubmed/28659508

9. https://www.ncbi.nlm.nih.gov/pubmed/?term=brogan+k+remote+healing

EVALUATING THE AUTHOR'S ARGUMENTS:

In this viewpoint, author Kelly Brogan, M.D., argues that people can treat some mental illnesses through methods other than prescription drugs. How does she support her assertion? Are you convinced that prescription drugs for mental illnesses are never needed, seldom needed, or often needed? Why?

Teens Suffer from Easy Access to Prescription Drugs

Margie Skeer

"Prescription drug misuse has been shown to increase the risk for further drug abuse, addiction and death by overdose."

In the following viewpoint, Margie Skeer addresses prescription drug abuse in teenagers. The author notes that prescription drug misuse is fairly common among teens. Many get the drugs from friends or relatives. Skeer discusses the factors that lead teens to either misuse or avoid the misuse of prescription drugs. Finally, she notes some ways drug abuse can be discouraged. Margie Skeer is an associate professor at Tufts University's School of Medicine. She researches substance misuse.

AS YOU READ, CONSIDER THE FOLLOWING QUESTIONS:

1. What prescription drugs are commonly misused by teenagers?
2. What factors contribute to prescription drug use by teenagers?
3. How does the use of recreational prescription drugs affect students' grades?

W hen you think about substance use and teens, drugs like marijuana or Ecstasy might come to mind. But recreational prescription drug use is a significant problem. Nationally, 17.8% of high school students have used prescription drugs without a prescription in their lifetime and 7% have done so at least ten times. The most common prescription drugs adolescents misuse are narcotics like Vicodin or stimulants like Adderall and Ritalin.

Prescription drug misuse has been shown to increase the risk for further drug abuse, addiction and death by overdose. In 2013, 1.5 million young people initiated non-medical use of pain relievers, which was second only to marijuana. Also, between 2004 and 2013, the number of people, both adolescents and adults, dependent on pain relievers rose from 1.4 to 1.9 million. To put that in perspective, in the US, overdoses outnumber traffic-related deaths.

As a researcher in the field of substance use and addiction, I wanted to know more about the risk factors for prescription drug misuse in teens. Colleagues and I reviewed the research on non-medical use of prescription drugs among teens and compiled a list of the strongest risk factors for misuse.

Risk Factors

We found that previous use of other illegal substances can be a risk factor because it could be related to a desire to experiment or the perception that drug use in general is not a big deal. Young people who do not think that using prescription drugs is harmful are more likely to use them for non-medical reasons than those who view them as harmful. Many young people think that prescription drugs are safer than other drugs because they are legal and prescribed by a doctor.

Greater access to prescription drugs also increases the chances of use. Doctors are prescribing an increasing number of prescription drugs in the US. Over the past two decades, there has been a three-fold increase in opioid prescriptions and a major increase in stimulant prescriptions given out by pharmacies nationally. This means teens are more likely to know someone with a prescription for these drugs, or are more likely to have them in their home.

For many teens, accessing prescription narcotics is all too easy.

Little Pills with Big Consequences

The 2013 Monitoring the Future report, a yearly survey of adolescent behavior and attitudes, revealed that over half of 12th grade students surveyed reported that it would be "fairly easy" or "very easy" to get prescription narcotic drugs (eg,

Vicodin, OxyContin, Percocet), saying that friends and relatives would be the primary source. Narcotic pain relievers and stimulants used to treat Attention Deficit Hyperactivity Disorder (ADHD) are the most commonly misused prescription drugs among young people. The use of Adderall and Ritalin has almost doubled in use since 2008. These drugs can provide a high or are perceived to increase attention and focus.

In general, high school students who report recreational prescription drug use tend to have worse grades and are more likely to drop out of school than their non-using peers. This is also the case for college students. Taking these drugs without a prescription or medical need may be due, in part, to students wanting to perform better in a competitive academic environment.

Teen Drug Use Is on a Downward Trend

Fortunately, the US is making strides in reducing substance misuse, especially among teenagers. Over the past decade, there has been a decline in alcohol, cigarette and illicit drug use among high school students, and the misuse of prescription drugs was down from 20.7% in 2011 to 17.8% in 2013.

Because many different factors can influence whether adolescents misuse prescription drugs, prevention and intervention programs need to address this problem from various angles. Reducing access to prescription drugs among adolescents and working with parents, pediatricians, teachers and coaches are good places to start. We should also encourage parents to discuss the harms of recreational drug use with their kids to help change adolescents' social norms and perceptions that prescription drugs are safer than other illegal drugs.

Those who play an important role in young people's lives can be influential when it comes to substance use. For example, having friends who use substances or approve of substance use can increase the chances that adolescents will misuse prescription drugs. In fact, this is one of strongest and most consistent risk factors for prescription drug misuse.

In our research we found a number of factors that seems to protect teens from prescription drug misuse. Parents who disapprove of substance use and play an active role in their children's lives can reduce the risk of their children using prescription drugs (and other substances) recreationally. We also found that young people who go to religious services frequently are less likely to use prescription drugs non-medically.

EVALUATING THE AUTHOR'S ARGUMENTS:

Author Margie Skeer notes that many teens do not think prescription drugs are as dangerous as illegal drugs. Based on this viewpoint, can you tell if that is true or not? Does your opinion change if you think about previous viewpoints in this book?

Viewpoint 3

Overprescribing Antibiotics Can Be Dangerous

Barry Segal

"As we try to 'stay clean' we move towards the destruction of the microbiome and the rise of chronic illness."

In the following viewpoint, Barry Segal explores the overuse of antibiotics. These medicines, which fight bacterial infections, have saved millions of lives. However, many bacteria have developed resistance to antibiotics. This leads to even more deadly infections. Antibiotic resistance happens when drugs are overprescribed. The drugs kill off not only the bad bacteria, but also good microorganisms. This can lead to chronic health issues. Barry Segal is a founder of the Focus for Health Foundation. This group promotes education and research to combat the rise of chronic illness around the world.

AS YOU READ, CONSIDER THE FOLLOWING QUESTIONS:
1. How do bacteria evolve to resist antibiotics?
2. How do antibiotics get into our diet and also into the environment?
3. What health problems can be blamed on the overuse of antibiotics, according to the viewpoint?

"The Pros and Cons of Prescription Drugs (series): Antibiotics," by Barry Segal, Focus for Health. Reprinted by permission.

Although antibiotics revolutionized medicine in the 20th century, and have saved countless lives, their overuse has led to some pretty scary consequences. Antibiotic resistance has become a dangerous public health dilemma, and the inadvertent alteration of our microbiome may be causing more health issues than previously realized.

Why Everyone Should Be Worried About Antibiotic Resistance

The World Health Organization has classified this problem as a "serious threat that is no longer a prediction for the future, it is happening right now—in every region of the world—with the potential to affect anyone, of any age, in any country."

Most people have heard the word "superbug." This is a layman's term encompassing many different types of bacteria that have developed resistance to multiple antibiotics. People who are exposed to these infections are left without medications that work for them, and the results can be life-threatening. The CDC estimates that about 2 million people develop these infections every year.

What Makes a Superbug?

The superbug we hear about most often is MRSA, or Methicillin-resistant Staphylococcus aureus. MRSA is a type of bacterial Staph infection that has learned how to evade not only Methicillin, but most of our currently available antibiotics. This type of infection kills more people every year than HIV/AIDS, and it is far from being the only one out there. Bacteria have developed some type of resistance to every antibiotic in existence.

Superbugs are known to medical professionals as MDRO's, or multi-drug resistant organisms, and they didn't just pop up overnight. Bacteria have always been great little evolvers. Within ten years of the introduction of the original antibiotic, penicillin, resistant strains began showing up in hospitals, and it didn't take long for these tricky organisms to figure out how to survive the next generation of medications.

The invention of the antibiotic is one of modern medicine's greatest achievements. However, overreliance on the drug has come at a cost.

The More People Use Antibiotics, the Faster They Evolve

Human beings evolve by natural selection. Spontaneous mutations happen in our DNA, and if that random change helps a person survive, then it will be passed on to the next generation. Bacteria do this also, but unlike us, they go beyond this process, and actually transfer DNA directly from one cell to another. If one little bacteria mutates an ability to elude eradication by a medication, then it can pass that survival information on to other bacteria nearby.

Keeping It Under Control

When these "smarter" bacteria multiply, they can cause serious infections. One way to prevent them from developing is to keep the use of all antibiotics to a minimum. Unfortunately, doctors are still way over-prescribing. A 2014 study published by the American Academy of Pediatrics found that over 11 million antibiotic prescriptions for kids could safely be avoided every year. According to the CDC, 50% of antibiotic prescriptions are unnecessary.

It is important to keep in mind that antibiotics do nothing to ease or prevent viral infections. Viruses include colds, flu, most sore throats and coughs, and most stomach bugs. When doctors prescribe medications to fight them, the virus is unaffected, but a potentially harmful side effects occurs—the good bacteria that are working to protect the body can be killed off in the process.

We cannot, as consumers, rely on physicians to always make the right choice. Many health care providers subscribe to a "better safe than sorry" philosophy, under the false belief that it is more harmful to do nothing than to do too much. There is recent evidence, however, that challenges this doctrine.

Antibiotics vs. Bacteria: What Really Keeps Us in Good Health?

We all understand that environmental factors can negatively affect our health, but it is also crucial to appreciate how the environment inside of the body influences our response to these external assaults.

Human beings engage in a perpetual battle with microorganisms, much of which goes completely unnoticed. Our bodies are home to ten times more bacteria than human cells, and these foreign organisms maintain a balancing act that helps to keep more harmful microbes from growing unchecked and causing illness.

Antibiotics come in many forms. They are prescribed as pills, given to livestock, added to household cleaners, and sprayed on crops that we eat. The intention is to kill harmful bacteria in order to keep infectious disease at bay, but the end result can be something very different. All of these exposures impact the approximately 100 trillion bacterial cells that colonize every human body, especially the "good bacteria" that thrive in our intestines. As we try to "stay clean," we move towards a very different, and more frightening, consequence: the destruction of the microbiome and the rise of chronic illness.

Chronic Illness and Gut Bacteria—A Case for Caution

Changing gut bacteria has been implicated by researchers as a possible cause of many chronic health issues, especially in children.

Use of antibiotics in early childhood has been linked to both asthma and the gastrointestinal disorder known as Crohn's disease. Repeated use of antibiotics in children has also been associated with obesity and the development of Type II diabetes. In mouse models, antibiotics accelerated the development of Type I diabetes, a disease that usually begins in childhood. Other research points to irresponsible use of antibiotics as a catalyst for Celiac disease, food allergies, reflux, and even autoimmune disorders, all of which have been on the rise since antibiotic use has increased.

Adult health can be equally affected. Many recent studies point to our gut bacteria as a significant factor in the development of many immune-mediated disorders like multiple sclerosis and rheumatoid arthritis.

Although it would be unreasonable to blame all chronic illness on the over-use of antibiotics, prudent use would undoubtedly have a positive effect on over-all health.

Next time your doctor offers you or your child a prescription, keep the microbiome in mind. Microbes like bacteria are not the enemy. Protecting our health should be focused on keeping the body in balance with optimal nutrition, decreased stress, and getting enough rest to restore immune function.

EVALUATING THE AUTHOR'S ARGUMENTS:

In this viewpoint, author Barry Segal argues that antibiotic use can have serious negative effects. Do you think the answer is to reduce or completely stop the use of antibiotics? Why? Is there other information you might want before making a decision?

Making Drugs Harder to Get Isn't the Answer

Ian Hamilton and Harry Sumnall

"Banning or restricting the supply of drugs can produce unintended consequences."

In the following viewpoint, Ian Hamilton and Harry Sumnall address the use of two common prescription drugs. Many people use these drugs in ways for which they were not prescribed. People may also combine the legal drugs with illegal drugs, which is dangerous. The government response to prescription drug abuse is often to make those drugs harder to get. This can be done by reclassifying the drugs to a different level of controlled substance. However, this typically only causes people to find different drugs to use. Ian Hamilton is an associate professor at the University of York, in the UK. Harry Sumnall is a professor in substance use at Liverpool John Moores University, in the UK.

AS YOU READ, CONSIDER THE FOLLOWING QUESTIONS:
1. Why might people mix prescription and illegal drugs?
2. What tends to happen when a drug is made harder to obtain?
3. Why is education not successful in preventing drug abuse?

Gabapentin and pregabalin, two widely used prescription drugs, are now subject to increased controls in the UK, which means they are now reclassified as class C controlled substances.

These drugs are licensed to treat epilepsy, anxiety, peripheral and neuropathic pain (pain caused by damage or injury to the nerves), but they are known to produce feelings of euphoria, calmness and relaxation. It is this mixed profile of effects that has contributed to their wide use. But these drugs can also have serious side effects, especially when combined with other drugs—and have been associated with use of illicit street drugs.

Under the new classification, prescribers can no longer issue electronic prescriptions—they will have to be handwritten. It is also now illegal to possess these drugs without a prescription, and it is illegal to supply or sell the drugs to others.

The Advisory Council on the Misuse of Drugs (ACMD), the government's independent scientific advisers, alerted the Home Office to a growing illicit market and the potential harms these drugs were causing. A 2016 ACMD report into these type of drugs highlighted that prescriptions for pregabalin had increased by 350% in the preceding five years and by 150% for gabapentin.

Although not as popular as other illicit drugs, there were particular concerns about their use in prisons, where there was a high number of prescriptions, as well in some parts of the UK such as Northern Ireland. Accompanying this was an alarming rise in deaths associated with their use.

One reason these drugs are particularly harmful is through the practice of combining them with other drugs to amplify the desired effects. For example, using gabapentin and pregabalin with heroin can increase their euphoric effects. Unfortunately, this also increases the risk of harm, as the combination can create breathing difficulties and reverse the tolerance that the body may have built up against heroin's effects on breathing. This increases the risk of respiratory failure, which underpins many heroin overdose deaths.

The potential misuse of gabapentin and pregabalin has been known about for some time, but the challenge has been how to respond and reduce harm. This is not the first prescribed medication

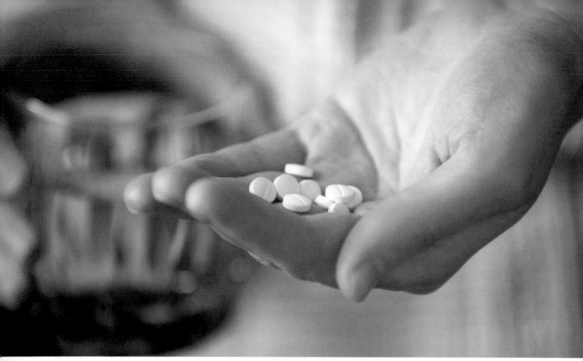

Government restriction of a supply of drugs can have unintended consequences.

to be reclassified in this way. Tramadol, a synthetic opiate, was made a class C drug in 2014. The circumstances leading up to this change were very similar to the concerns relating to gabapentin, namely an increase in prescriptions, which was accompanied by a rise in fatalities.

Since the reclassification of tramadol, deaths have fallen as have the number of prescriptions. By this measure, it would appear that the reclassification decision for tramadol was a success. Unfortunately, it's not that straightforward.

Shifting Use

Banning or restricting the supply of drugs, whether they are legal or illegal, can produce unintended consequences. One of these is displacement, where tightening up access to one substance shifts use onto another.

It is possible that this has happened with tramadol given the rise in use of gabapentin and pregabalin—as it became harder for people to obtain, they found gabapentin and pregabalin easier to get hold of, so they became desirable alternatives. This suggests that the new restrictions on gabapentin may move the problem onto another drug, although it is likely that it will be the same group of higher risk people who are most affected. The problem is we don't know which drug that will be, and we are unlikely to find out until the same prescribing and mortality data provide fresh information.

When we are assessing the impact of changes to drug laws, we shouldn't solely focus on what happens to the harms associated with the drug that is banned but whether the total burden of harm from all drugs has been affected. Data showing a very high level of drug-related deaths and hospitalisations suggests that we are failing to make much of an impact.

Most people who use these drugs know the risks they face, so thinking we can simply educate or arrest our way out of this problem is unlikely to be successful. People are often attracted to using these drugs to alleviate a range of problems beyond the physical, and they are often trying to mitigate psychological pain and social problems.

Accessing support for such issues has become increasingly difficult. Treatment services have faced budget cuts that restrict their ability to respond quickly. Little surprise then that people turn to drugs that have no waiting lists, can be accessed 24 hours a day and where dealers don't ask intrusive questions.

EVALUATING THE AUTHORS' ARGUMENTS:

In this viewpoint, authors Ian Hamilton and Harry Sumnall note that when the government reclassifies drugs to make them harder to get, people find other drugs to abuse. The authors also suggest that education doesn't work. Does this mean it's impossible to stop drug abuse? Why or why not? If making drugs harder to get isn't the answer, what might be?

Misusing Drugs Can Be Deadly

US Food and Drug Administration

"People just like you are dropping pills at parties and dropping dead."

In the following viewpoint, authors at the US Food and Drug Administration aim to teach young people the dangers of misusing drugs. The authors warn that prescription drugs can be deadly if misused, especially if combined with other drugs. The viewpoint then lists signs that indicate someone had taken a dangerous overdose. It offers advice on how to make sure friends don't overdose and die. Finally, it mentions the danger of addiction. The US Food and Drug Administration is responsible for protecting the public health by ensuring the safety of drugs and other products.

AS YOU READ, CONSIDER THE FOLLOWING QUESTIONS:
1. When are prescription pain relievers safe?
2. Why is it important not to let a friend go to sleep if they have been misusing drugs?
3. What is the best way to get anonymous help for someone who may be suffering from an overdose?

How many times has someone told you a "party" drug could lead to more serious problems—like addiction, brain damage, or even death? You've probably heard it so many

"Misuse of Prescription Pain Relievers: The Buzz Takes Your Breath Away . . . Permanently," US Food and Drug Administration, January 10, 2018.

Experimenting with drugs recreationally, even prescription drugs, is never worth the risk involved.

times, it's getting hard to believe. Especially when kids around you are smoking, drinking, and rolling. But all drugs have real potential for harm—even prescription pain relievers. When abused alone, or taken with other drugs, prescription pain medications can kill you. And the death toll from misuse and abuse is rising steadily.

Think Twice—Because You Only Die Once

Prescription pain relievers, when used correctly and under a doctor's supervision, are safe and effective. But abuse them, or mix them with illegal drugs or alcohol, and you could wind up in the morgue. Even using prescription pain relievers with other prescription drugs (such as antidepressants) or over-the-counter medications (like cough syrups and antihistamines) can lead to life-threatening respiratory failure. That's why people just like you are dropping pills at parties, and dropping dead. They're not downing handfuls of pills, either. With some prescription pain relievers, all it takes is one pill.

Drugs to Watch Out For

The most dangerous prescription pain relievers are those containing drugs known as opioids, such as morphine and codeine. Some common drugs containing these substances include Darvon, Demerol, Dilaudid, OxyContin, Tylenol with Codeine, and Vicodin. Your friends probably call these drugs by their street names: ac/dc, coties, demmies, dillies, hillbilly heroin, o.c., oxy, oxycotton, percs and vics to name a few. Whatever you call them, remember one thing—they can be killers.

Symptoms of Overdose

If you, or any of your friends, have taken prescription pain relievers, here are the danger signs to watch for:

- Slow breathing (less than ten breaths a minute is really serious trouble)
- Small, pinpoint pupils
- Confusion
- Being tired, nodding off, or passing out
- Dizziness

- Weakness
- Apathy (they don't care about anything)
- Cold and clammy skin
- Nausea
- Vomiting
- Seizures

A lot of these symptoms can make people think your friend is drunk. And you may be tempted to let them sleep it off, or tell their parents they had too much to drink. But don't. Your friend could go to sleep and never wake up.

What You Can Do If a Friend Is Overdosing

Make an anonymous call to 911 or your friend's parents if you're too scared to identify yourself. Try to get your friend to respond to you by calling out his/her name. Make your friend wake up and talk to you. Shake him/her if you have to. Otherwise, your friend could suffer brain damage, fall into a coma, or die.

Addiction Can Be a Living Death

If you abuse prescription pain relievers and are lucky enough to cheat death, you're still in big trouble. Prescription pain relievers can be addictive. The longer you take them, the more your body needs. Try to stop, and you could experience withdrawal symptoms.

Addiction to prescription pain relievers is like being hooked on heroin and the withdrawal isn't much different: bone and muscle pain, diarrhea, vomiting, cold flashes and insomnia.

If you, or someone you know, is abusing or is addicted, get professional help. You can also ask for help from parents, doctors, relatives, teachers, or school guidance counselors. Substance abuse ruins lives. Don't let it happen to your friends—or you.

If you, or someone you know, is hooked on prescription pain relievers, call the substance abuse treatment 24-hour helpline: 1.800.662.HELP.

Facts About Prescription Drugs

Editor's note: These facts can be used in reports to add credibility when making important points or claims.

Getting Drugs to Market

The term **pharmaceutical** relates to drugs taken as medicine. A prescription drug can only be obtained with a prescription written by a medical practitioner. Over-the-counter drugs are available without a prescription.

In the United States, it takes about 12 years for an experimental drug to make it through testing and become available to patients. Only about 14 percent of all drugs in clinical trials are approved by the FDA.

Some figures claim that it costs on average $1.3 billion to develop a new drug and get it approved. This includes the cost of failures. It can include profits that companies would have made if they had invested their research money elsewhere. It includes tax deductions and credits. Statistics may also consider only the most expensive drugs. Calculating the expense in a different way brings the cost down as low as $125 million per successful new drug.

A **clinical study** uses human volunteers in research intended to add to medical knowledge. Clinical studies include clinical trials and observational studies.

Clinical trials are also called interventional studies. In a clinical trial, the volunteers may be asked to take drugs, use devices, or change their behavior. The results may be compared to current standard treatments, to a placebo with no active ingredients, or to a control group that does not make changes.

In an **observational study**, the study does not ask participants to make specific changes. They may receive drugs, medical products, or advice as part of their regular medical care. The study observes the participants over time to learn outcomes. For example, a study might look at the effects of diet on heart health.

Prescription Drug Spending

The United States is the largest single pharmaceutical market. The United States holds 5 percent of the world's population, but it accounts for 42 percent of global prescription drug spending.

Nearly 70 percent of Americans take at least one prescription drug. About one in four Americans have trouble paying for their prescription drugs. They may skip medications or take less than the prescribed amount.

According to a February 2017 article in the *Los Angeles Times,* drug companies spend more than $5 billion a year pitching prescription medications directly to consumers.

Pharmaceutical companies spend $19 on advertising a new drug for every one dollar spent on research and development. Every $1 spent advertising prescription drugs is estimated to increase their sales by $4.20.

Direct-to-consumer advertising of prescription drugs is only legal in the US and New Zealand.

Drug Addiction and Dependence

Dependence happens when the body adapts to regularly taking a medication. Stopping the medication can cause withdrawal symptoms. For example, according to the Addiction Center, "Antidepressant dependence can form in people who never needed the drugs in the first place. Some people are incorrectly diagnosed with depression and prescribed antidepressants. According to one study, doctors misdiagnosed almost two-thirds of patients with depression and prescribed unnecessary antidepressants." Those patients may then become dependent on antidepressants and suffer withdrawal symptoms if they abruptly stop using them. Slowly tapering off use can typically prevent withdrawal.

Addiction is a brain disease that causes people to use substances or engage in behaviors despite harmful consequences. People take drugs by choice at first. However, the drugs cause changes in parts of the brain that affect judgment, behavior control, decision making, learning, and memory. The person may then intensely crave drugs. They may continue using drugs even when that use is severely damaging their life. Addiction is a complex medical illness that can be treated with medications and behavioral therapy.

For a complete list of drug addiction symptoms, see "The Science of Drug Use and Addiction: The Basics," from the National Institute on Drug Abuse at https://www.drugabuse.gov/publications/media-guide/science-drug-use-addiction-basics.

Drug toxicity can happen when a patient takes too much of a drug. The liver or kidneys cannot remove the drug from the bloodstream, so it builds up in the body. This most often happens when a patient takes too high a dose, either intentionally or accidentally. In some cases, a normal dose may be toxic for a particular patient.

Drug classifications organize drugs into categories. Many countries have legal classification systems. However, even experts often disagree about how drugs should be classified. In the US, the Controlled Substances Act established five drug classifications, or "schedules." Schedule V drug have the fewest regulations. They are thought to have low potential for addiction and abuse, and a legitimate medical purpose. Schedule I drugs have the most regulations and harshest penalties. They have no accepted medical use and a high potential for abuse.

According to the Centers for Disease Control, 70,237 drug overdose deaths occurred in the United States in 2017. Of those deaths, about 68 percent involved a prescription or illicit opioid. Opioids include the illegal drug heroin, along with pain relievers available legally by prescription. These pain relievers include codeine, morphine, oxycodone (OxyContin), hydrocodone (Vicodin), and many others.

Organizations to Contact

The editors have compiled the following list of organizations concerned with the issues debated in this book. The descriptions are derived from materials provided by the organizations. All have publications or information available for interested readers. The list was compiled on the date of publication of the present volume; the information provided here may change. Be aware that many organizations take several weeks or longer to respond to inquiries, so allow as much time as possible for the receipt of requested materials.

Alliance of Community Health Plans (ACHP)

1825 Eye Street NW, Suite 401
Washington, DC 20006
(202) 785-2247
contact form: https://achp.org/about-us/contact-us
website: achp.org
ACHP is dedicated to tackling the high cost of prescription drugs. See the "Advocacy" page for information on prescription drugs.

Food and Drug Administration (FDA)

5600 Fishers Lane
Rockville, MD 20857-0001
(888) INFO-FDA
email: druginfo@fda.hhs.gov
website: https://www.fda.gov
The US FDA is responsible for protecting public health by ensuring the safety of drugs, medical devices, and more. Learn what products the FDA regulates, including drugs, tobacco products, cosmetics, and food, and explore current research.

Nar-Anon

23110 Crenshaw Boulevard, Suite A
Torrance, CA 90505
(800) 477-6291
email: wso@nar-anon.org

website: www.nar-anon.org

Nar-Anon is for those who are affected by a loved one's addiction. Narateen is designed for teen Nar-Anon members. Find a group, learn how to start a group, and subscribe to the quarterly newsletter.

The National Academy for State Health Policy (NASHP)

1233 20th Street NW, Suite 303
Washington, DC 20036
(202) 903-0101
website: nashp.org/policy/prescription-drug-pricing

NASHP works with state governments to address health policy challenges. The website provides news updates and a tracking system to keep up with state legislative action to lower pharmaceutical costs.

National Coalition Against Prescription Drug Abuse (NCAPDA)

PO Box 87
San Ramon, CA 94583
(925) 480-7723
email: info@ncapda.org
website: ncapda.org

NCAPDA's mission is to prevent addiction and overdose deaths related to prescription drug abuse. Learn about signs of addiction and ways to get involved.

National Institute on Drug Abuse (NIDA)

6001 Executive Boulevard, Room 5213
Bethesda, MD 20892-9561
(301) 443-1124
website: www.drugabuse.gov

NIDA, part of the US National Institutes of Health, states as its mission: "to advance science on the causes and consequences of drug use and addiction and to apply that knowledge to improve individual and public health." Learn about commonly abused drugs and emerging trends.

Substance Abuse and Mental Health Services Administration (SAMHSA)
5600 Fishers Lane
Rockville, MD 20857
(301) 443-5052
email: media@samhsa.hhs.gov
website: www.samhsa.gov
SAMHSA leads public health efforts to advance behavioral health. The website covers current topics, helps people find treatments, and has a newsroom of up-to-date articles.

White House Office of National Drug Control Policy (ONDCP)
PO Box 6000
Rockville, MD 20849-6000
(800) 666-3332
website: www.whitehouse.gov/ondcp
ONDCP coordinates the development, implementation, and assessment of US drug policy. The website focuses on the government's attempts to end the opioid crisis.

Young People in Recovery (YPR)
1415 Park Avenue West
Denver, CO 80205-2103
(720) 600-4977
contact form: youngpeopleinrecovery.org/contact
website: youngpeopleinrecovery.org
YPR provides life skills and peer support to help young people recover from substance use disorders.

For Further Reading

Books

Bodden, Valerie, and Sarah T. Melton. *Prescription and Over-the-Counter Drugs*. Minneapolis, MN: Essential Library, 2019. This book explores how prescription and over-the-counter drugs affect the body, the laws surrounding these drugs, and their impact on society.

Brand, Russell. *Recovery: Freedom from Our Addictions*. New York, NY: Henry Holt and Co., 2017. A comedian and movie star shares his struggle with addiction and provides a recovery plan.

Braun, Eric. *Big Pharma and the Opioid Epidemic: From Vicodin to Heroin*. North Mankato, MN: Compass Point Books, 2020. This book examines the opioid epidemic in the United States, a national crisis. It also offers practical advice for helping someone who has an addiction or who has overdosed.

Brogan, Kelly, M.D. *A Mind of Your Own*. New York, NY: Harper Wave, 2016. A holistic doctor (the author of Chapter 3, Viewpoint 1) argues that antidepressants are not the answer to depression. She suggests alternative methods, including lifestyle changes.

Bryant, Robert L., and Howard L. Forman, M.D. *Prescription Drug Abuse (Health and Medical Issues Today)*. Westport, CT: Greenwood, 2019. This book explores the risks and controversies surrounding prescription drug abuse. Case studies highlight key ideas and debates.

Eban, Katherine. *Bottle of Lies: The Inside Story of the Generic Drug Boom*. New York, NY: Ecco, 2019. A journalist provides "an explosive narrative investigation of the generic drug boom that reveals fraud and life-threatening dangers on a global scale."

Feldman, Robin. *Drugs, Money, and Secret Handshakes: The Unstoppable Growth of Prescription Drug Prices*. Cambridge, UK: Cambridge University Press, 2019. Dive into the "warped world" of prescription drug pricing and learn how the pharmaceutical industry promotes expensive drugs over cheap ones.

Feldman, Robin. *Drug Wars: How Big Pharma Raises Prices and Keeps Generics Off the Market.* Cambridge, UK: Cambridge University Press, 2017. A study of the inner workings of the pharmaceutical industry. Learn how companies create barriers to competition from generic drugs.

Ferguson, Grace. *Chronic Pain and Prescription Painkillers.* Broomall, PA: Mason Crest, 2018. This book explores the marketing and promotion of opioids by pharmaceutical companies and evaluates the steps taken by legislative bodies to balance the problem of chronic pain and prescription opioid abuse.

Hanson, Glen R. *Drugs and Society.* Burlington, MA: Jones & Bartlett Learning, 2017. A look at drug use and abuse on the lives of average people. The title includes personal experiences and institutional perspectives.

Pierce, Simon. *Prescription Drugs: Opioids That Kill.* New York, NY: Lucent Press, 2017. This book emphasizes the potential dangers of prescription drugs.

Poole, Hilary W. *Prescription Drugs.* Broomall, PA: Mason Crest, 2017. This book discusses the history and effects of painkillers, sedatives, hypnotics, stimulants, and other commonly prescribed medications that are often subject to abuse.

Schauer, Pete. *Big Pharma and Drug Pricing* (Opposing Viewpoints). Farmington Hills, MI: Greenhaven Press, 2018. This title covers conflicts and potential solutions for high prescription drug prices.

Spiegelman, Erica. *Rewired: A Bold New Approach to Addiction and Recovery.* Hobart, NY: Hatherleigh Press, 2015. An approach to fighting addiction that includes inspiring stories and questions to engage the reader.

Periodicals and Internet Sources

"Antibiotic Resistance," World Health Organization, February 5, 2018. https://www.who.int/news-room/fact-sheets/detail/antibiotic-resistance

"The Dangers of Misused Prescription Drugs," ULifeline. http://www.ulifeline.org/articles/390-the-dangers-of-misused-prescription-drugs

"Do Generic Drugs Compromise on Quality?" *Harvard Health Publishing*, January 2018. https://www.health.harvard.edu/staying-healthy/do-generic-drugs-compromise-on-quality

"The Pros and Cons of Prescription Drugs (series): Antibiotics," Focus for Health. https://www.focusforhealth.org/antibiotics-both-good-and-bad

"Should Prescription Drugs Be Advertised Directly to Consumers?" ProCon.org. https://prescriptiondrugs.procon.org

Emanuel, Ezekiel J., "Big Pharma's Go-To Defense of Soaring Drug Prices Doesn't Add Up," *Atlantic*, March 23, 2019. https://www.theatlantic.com/health/archive/2019/03/drug-prices-high-cost-research-and-development/585253

Greenwood, Jim, "The Right Way to Address Prescription Drug Costs," *STAT*, December 20, 2018. https://www.statnews.com/2018/12/20/right-way-address-prescription-drug-costs

Hassoun, Nicole, "How Can We Get Pharma Companies to Do More for Global Health? Try Ranking Them," *Conversation*, September 21, 2016. https://theconversation.com/how-can-we-get-pharma-companies-to-do-more-for-global-health-try-ranking-them-62888

Johnson, Carolyn Y., "Expensive Specialty Drugs Are Forcing Seniors to Make Hard Choices," *Washington Post*, November 10, 2017. https://www.washingtonpost.com/news/wonk/wp/2017/11/10/expensive-specialty-drugs-are-forcing-seniors-to-make-hard-choices

Joyce, Michael, "Consumer Drug Ads: The Harms That Come with Pitching Lifestyle over Information," *Health News Review*, May 23, 2018. https://www.healthnewsreview.org/2018/05/direct-to-consumer-tv-drug-ads

Kelley, Timothy, "When the Cost of Medications Keeps Patients from Taking Them," *Managed Care*, June 3, 2018. https://www.managedcaremag.com/archives/2018/6/when-cost-medications-keeps-patients-taking-them

Kliff, Sarah, "The True Story of America's Sky-High Prescription Drug Prices," *Vox*, May 10, 2018. https://www.vox.com/science-and-health/2016/11/30/12945756/prescription-drug-prices-explained

Leahy, James, "There's a Way for Modern Medicine to Cure Diseases Even When the Treatments Aren't Profitable," *Conversation*, September 16, 2019. https://theconversation.com/theres-a-way-for-modern-medicine-to-cure-diseases-even-when-the-treatments-arent-profitable-122294

LeWine, Howard, "Millions of Adults Skip Medications Due to Their High Cost," Harvard Health Publishing, January 30, 2015. https://www.health.harvard.edu/blog/millions-skip-medications-due-to-their-high-cost-201501307673

Mayo Clinic Staff, "Prescription Drug Abuse," Mayo Foundation for Medical Education and Research (MFMER). https://www.mayoclinic.org/diseases-conditions/prescription-drug-abuse/symptoms-causes/syc-20376813

Ogbru, Omudhome, "Why Drugs Cost So Much," Medicine Net, June 13, 2018. https://www.medicinenet.com/drugs_why_drugs_cost_so_much/views.htm

ProCon.org, "Should Prescription Drugs Be Advertised Directly to Consumers?" ProCon.org, October 23, 2018. https://prescriptiondrugs.procon.org

Segal, Barry, "The Pros and Cons of Prescription Drugs (series): Antidepressants," Focus for Health. https://www.focusforhealth.org/depression-and-the-over-use-of-antidepressants-are-we-treating-the-real-problem

Sherwood, Ted, "The Generic Drug Approval Process," FDA, November 20, 2017. https://www.fda.gov/drugs/news-events-human-drugs/generic-drug-approval-process

Smith, Kathleen, "Prescription Drug Abuse," Psycom.net, November 25, 2018. https://www.psycom.net/prescription-drug-abuse

Websites
Addiction Center (www.addictioncenter.com)
This website allows visitors to learn about the different drugs that can cause addiction, health effects of addiction, and treatment options.

Heads Up for Students (headsup.scholastic.com)
Watch interactive videos, read straightforward drug facts, or take the "National Drug IQ Challenge."

National Institute on Drug Abuse (NIDA) for Teens (www .drugabuse.gov/children-and-teens)
Learn how different drugs affect your body and brain. Watch videos, or download informational graphics and statistics.

Patients for Affordable Drugs (www.patientsforaffordabledrugs.org)
This national patient organization focuses on achieving policy changes to lower the price of prescription drugs. Learn what's in the news, and read personal stories about people struggling to pay for prescription medicines.

Index

A
Adderall, 87, 89
addiction, finding help for, 103
Addiction Center, 9, 83
ADHD, 7, 8, 89
Advair, 74
advertising, money spent on, 20, 21, 27, 47, 70
Affordable Care Act, 76
alcohol, 16, 81, 83, 89, 102
amitriptyline, 14
Anatomy of an Epidemic, 83
antibiotics, overprescribing of, 9, 91–95
antidepressants, 9, 14, 80–85
Apple, 41
asthma, 7, 95
Azar, Alex, 45

B
Beier, David, 49–53
Boehringer Ingelheim, 39
Brogan, Kelly, 80–85
Brown, Sherrod, 46

C
cancer, 7, 47, 60–64
cannabis, medicinal, 14
CDC (Centers for Disease Control and Prevention), 92, 93
Children's Health Insurance Program, 76
chronic pain, treatment of with pain relievers, 11–17
clinical trials, and real-world data, 37–42
codeine, 14, 102
compulsory licensing, 51, 52

D
Darvon, 102
Demerol, 102
depression, 7, 9, 12, 80, 83
diabetes, 7, 95
diclofenac, 12, 14
Dilaudid, 102
DiMasi, Joseph A., 55, 57, 58–59
direct-to-consumer advertising, 18–22
diseases, creation and marketing of, 23–31
Doggett, Lloyd, 46
drug classifications/schedules, 99
drug toxicity, 32–36

E
Eli Lilly, 39, 69

F
Fayaz, Alan, 12, 14
Fischer, Mary A., 32–36
Fugh-Berman, Adriane, 24, 26, 28, 29

G

gabapentin, 14, 96–99
Gislason, Gunnar, 12, 14
GlaxoSmithKline, 40
Gottlieb, Scott, 40, 69
Grayson, Neile, 37–42
Greenwood, Jim, 49–53

H

Haeder, Simon F., 72–78
Hamilton, Ian, 96–99
health insurance, 7, 8, 44, 76
Health of Populations, The, 26
Heard, Kennon, 34
Hernandez, Inmaculada, 45
heroin, 81, 83, 97, 102, 103

I

ibuprofen, 11, 14
insulin, 66, 67–68
international reference
    pricing, 51

J

James, Jack, 26, 29–30, 31
Jones, Anthony, 15, 16

K

Kaiser Family
    Foundation, 45, 47
Kantarjian, Hagop, 60–64
Katz, Mitchell J., 27
Kodjak, Alison, 44–48

L

Light, Donald W., 60–64
Lipitor, 74
Love, James, 58

M

*Many People Taking
    Antidepressants Discover They
    Can't Quit,* 81
market spiral pricing strategy, 63
Medicaid, 76, 77
Medicare, 44–48, 50, 51, 52,
    63, 70, 76, 77
Medicare for All, 70
Medicare Part D, 76
Mind of Your Own, A, 80, 84
morphine, 14, 102
Murakami, Haruki, 12

N

naproxen, 14
National Cancer Institute, 63
National Women's Health
    Network, 30
NSAIDs, 12, 14

O

opioid epidemic, 24, 82
opioids, 14, 24, 82, 87, 102
orphan drugs, 75, 77
overdose, symptoms
    of, 102–103
overdoses/deaths, 8, 12, 87, 89,
    97, 98, 99, 100–104
OxyContin, 82, 89, 102

P

Packer, Milton, 18–22
pain relievers, use of to treat
    chronic pain, 11–17
Pearson, Cindy, 30–31
Percocet, 89

W

Walsh, Michael, 23–31
Warren, Elizabeth, 66–67, 70
Whitaker, Robert, 83
Williams, Laura, 65–71
Woloshin, Steven, 26, 28
World Health Organization
   (WHO), 9, 92

X

Xanax, 81, 82

Z

Zoloft, 81

Picture Credits

Cover fstop123/E+/Getty Images; pp. 10, 93 SDI Productions/E+/Getty Images; p. 13 Daisy-Daisy/Alamy Stock Photo; p. 20 iko/Shutterstock.com; p. 25 Tetra Images, LLC/Alamy Stock Photo; p. 34 © iStockphoto.com/fizkes; p. 39 hocus-focus/iStock Unreleased/Getty Images; pp. 43, 101 Juanmonino/E+/Getty Images; p. 46 Bloomberg/Getty Images; p. 51 Charly Triballeau/AFP/Getty Images; p. 56 AFP/Getty Images; p. 62 Pacific Press/LightRocket/Getty Images; p. 67 Syda Productions/Shutterstock.com; p. 74 Mangpink/Shutterstock.com; p. 79 Anakumka/Alamy Stock Photo; p. 82 baona/E+/Getty Images; p. 88 SW Productions/Photodisc/Getty Images; p. 98 fizkes/Shutterstock.com.